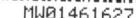

CELEBRITY WASHINGTON

CELEBRITY WASHINGTON

Who they are, where they live
and why they're famous

PLUS
Maps, Photos, Movie Locations and Restaurants

Jan Pottker

☆

Writer's Cramp Books

Copyright 1995 Writer's Cramp, Inc.

All rights reserved.
No part of this book may be reproduced in any form, by photostat, microfilm, xerography or any other means, or incorporated into any information retrieval system, electronic or mechanical, without permission of the copyright owner.

All inquiries should be addressed to:
Jan Pottker
Writer's Cramp Books
P.O. Box 60107
Potomac, Maryland 20854-0107
tel/fax (301) 762-3049 or out of area 800 775-8229

Manuscript preparation by
Black Bear Productions, Inc. (800) 530-1597

Library of Congress Catalog Card No. 95-90170

ISBN 0-9645983-0-2

PRINTED IN THE UNITED STATES OF AMERICA

First Edition

1 2 3 4 5 6 7 8 9 10

Jan Pottker is a Washington area writer who lives at 10104 Lloyd Road, Potomac, Maryland, around the corner from Ted Koppel. *Celebrity Washington* is her sixth book. Her fifth book was *Crisis in Candyland: Melting the Chocolate Shell of the Mars Family Empire*, National Press Books, 1995.

Many thanks go to Fiona Houston, who provided invaluable research assistance for this book. Grateful acknowledgement is also made to the Washingtoniana Room of the Martin Luther King Library, Washington DC; the Office of TV & Film, Washington DC; and to Peggy Pridemore, film location manager.

Questions, comments, corrections, additions?
Please telephone (301) 762-3049.
If your information is used, you will receive the 1997 edition of *Celebrity Washington* free.

To Washington, central star of the constellation, may it enlighten the whole world.

LAFAYETTE, 1824

CONTENTS

Maps	*ii*
Why Celebrity Washington?	*v*
Celebrity Washington's Quick Facts	*ix*
Media Stars	1
Clinton's Crowd	11
Politicos & Powerbrokers	15
SuperRich, Athletes & Entertainers	31
From the Past	39
Movie Locations	49
The Playing Fields	55
Index: By Name	*73*
By Neighborhood	*80*

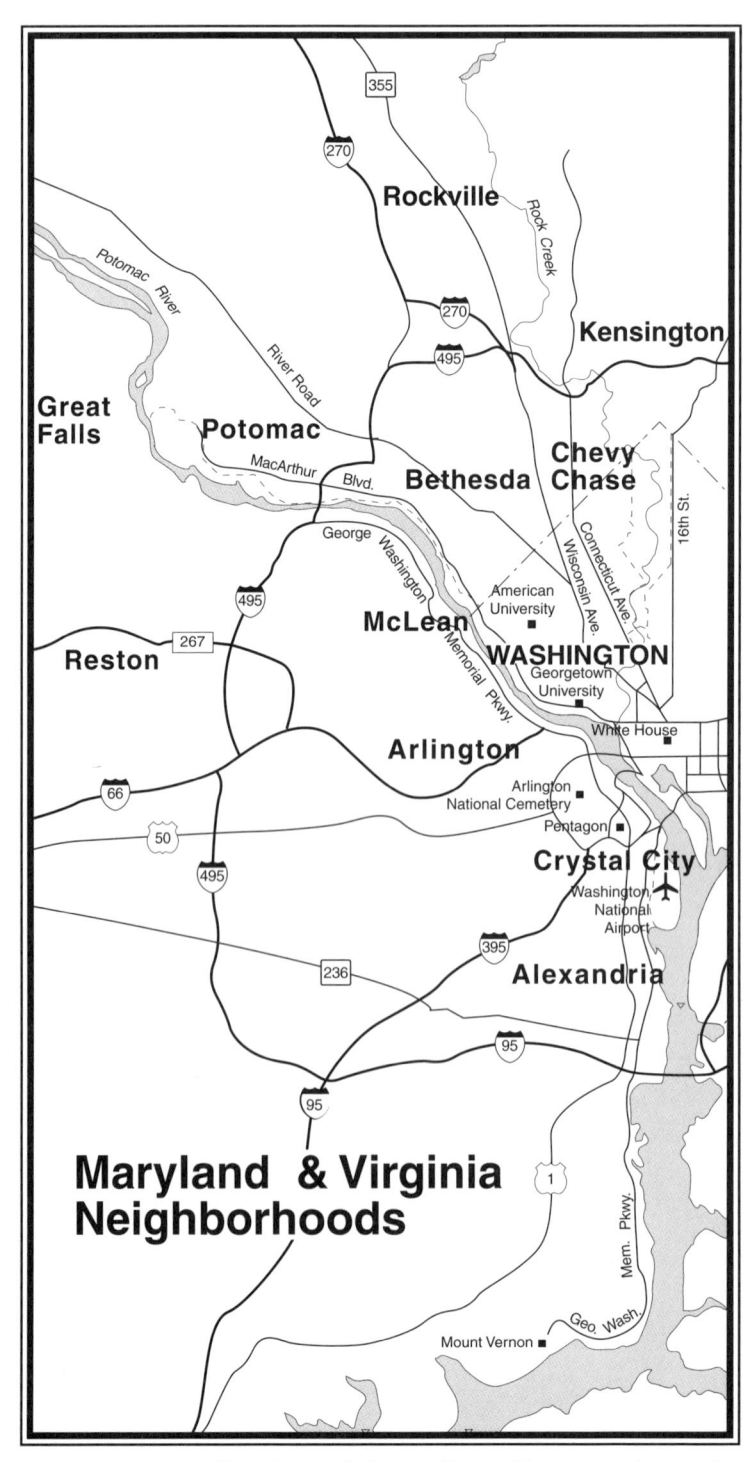

Map shows relative position and is not exactly to scale.

MAPS

Washington D.C. Neighborhoods

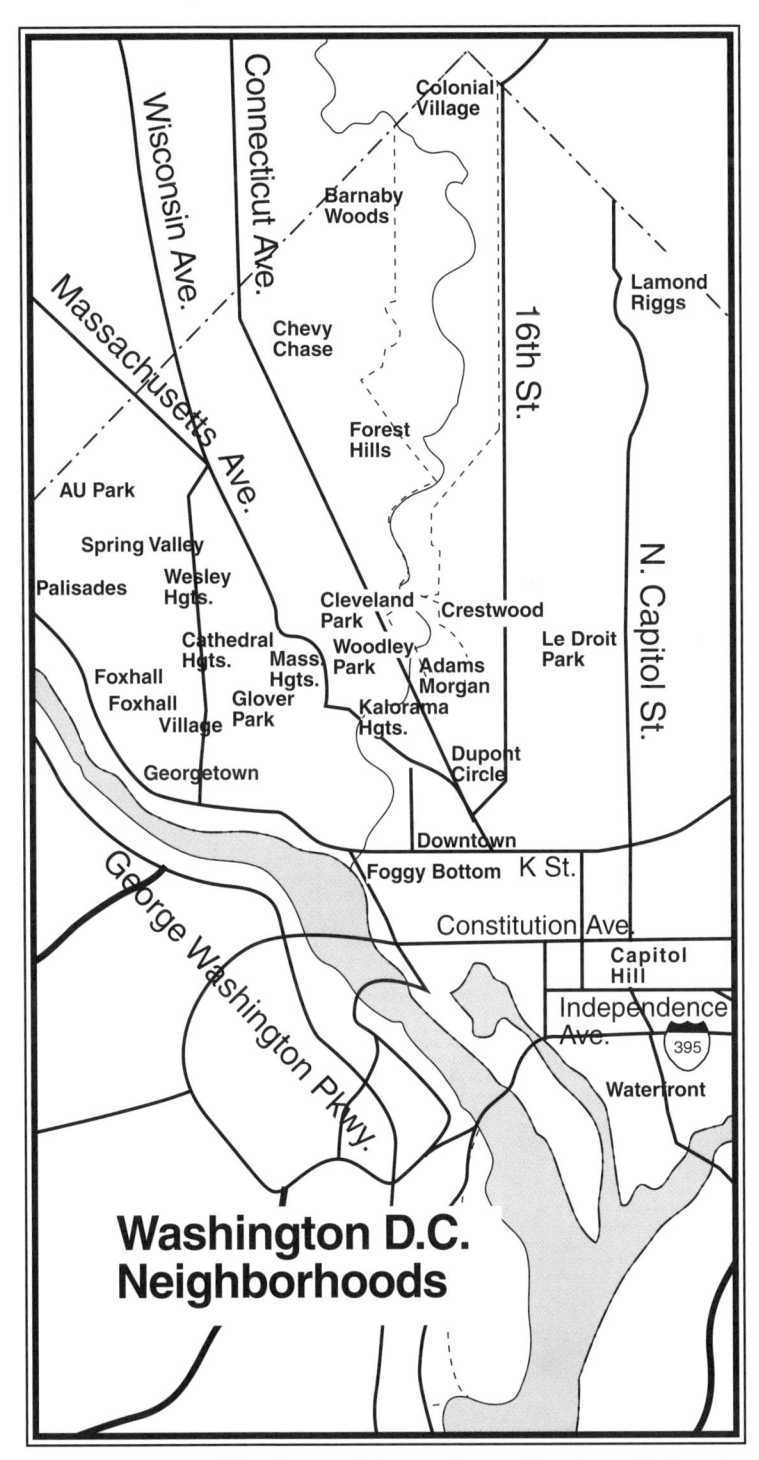

Map shows relative position and is not exactly to scale.

WHY CELEBRITY WASHINGTON?

Now, for the first time, metropolitan Washington has a guide to the stars. *Celebrity Washington* is the first handbook that identifies the area's current celebrities and gives their residential addresses. It is an address book for people who want to send a letter to a famous Washingtonian and it is a guidebook for those who are interested in viewing the houses and neighborhoods of the famous.

Celebrity Washington includes more than 300 celebrity listings with home addresses, as well as identifying where they eat and party. There's also a chapter giving the locations of scenes from recent movies shot in the Washington area.

I have been thinking about writing a residential guide to Washington's celebrities since the fall of 1966, when I left the midwest to attend college at American University. Blame the driver of the Yellow Cab that took me from National Airport over Key Bridge up Foxhall Road on my first trip to AU. I was a mesmerized freshman on that sunny autumn day, entranced by the houses and neighborhoods I passed through on my way up to Ward Circle.

Not that I was surprised by the wealth of Washington's residences. I grew up on Chicago's swank North Shore, so the neighborhoods of Highland Park, Lake Forest and Winnetka compared favorably to those of Kalorama, McLean and Georgetown. The main difference was that in the 50s and 60s, midwesterners were unknown except within their own social circle, whereas in Washington, it seemed to me then—and still does today—that there's a famous person living on every block of this town.

Maybe I was destined to write this guide, which is my sixth book, from the time of the leisurely Sunday drives my family used to take when I was a girl growing up in Highland Park. These impromptu outings may not seem unusual, but our frequent destination certainly was. Our preferred site was one of the local cemeteries that served the wealthy. As the Pottker family lazily cruised through lush burial grounds in our four-door Dodge, with Dad driving, Mom in the front passenger seat and my older sister Mary Helene and me jostling in the back seat, we would be thrilled to spot an imposing monument. Then we would park, jump out and race to read the inscription: was it the mausoleum of a meat-packing Armour, whose business greed was immortalized in Upton Sinclair's *The Jungle*?

v

Was it the grave of one of the Rosenwalds of Sears & Roebuck, whose relative was of Leopold and Loeb murder fame? Sometimes we'd locate a double-barreled name: Abigail Rockefeller McCormick was a great find. I'd gaze in awe up at the grey stone memorial that dwarfed me and hear the stories my parents would tell about the great deeds—or scandals—of the past.

Afterward, we'd drive out of the cemetery, discussing which tombstone indicated the greatest wealth and which name was the most famous, while we looked for a Good Humor ice cream truck to treat ourselves to a Toasted Almond or Chocolate Eclair bar.

It never occurred to me that these trips might be considered somewhat macabre. Instead, what stayed with me was the notion that the rich are more vivid than the middle-class, even in death. That's probably what led me to study sociology, which examines how a person's education, income and social position determines behavior. In fact, the several years I took for course work to earn a Ph.D. degree from Columbia University was the only time I have lived outside the Washington area in nearly three decades.

And, loving Washington, I could not fathom why the most important city in the world lacked a guidebook to its own celebrities and their addresses. Los Angeles boasts a dozen guides, with such titles as *The Ultimate Hollywood Tour Book, This is Hollywood: An Unusual Movieland Guide* and, even, *The L.A. Musical History Tour.* New York City also has guidebooks to celebrities' residences: *Movie Stars' Homes* and *New York City Starwalks,* both by Larry "The Star Sleuth" Horowitz, can be found in any Manhattan bookstore.

To be sure, there are already specialized guides to famous and infamous Washingtonians. *Literary Washington* by David Cutler and *Undercover Washington* by Pamela Kessler are excellent guides for identifying local writers or for leading readers to the sites where famous spies lived, worked and loved.

But I thought it was high time to expose the home addresses of real celebrities: people who are known, not from their membership in a specialized group, but whose names are nationally—and internationally—recognized. And I wanted *Celebrity Washington* to identify the actual home addresses of these stars. I had always been frustrated by the celebrity house photos that run in local newspapers and magazines. These publications give a glimpse of a celebrity house, maybe even mention its neighborhood, but don't print the specific address. I wanted *Celebrity Washington* to come through with the real goods. After all, the people at the newspaper have this information; it seems elitist to assume that it should be kept from the public, as the details of politicians' personal lives used to be.

Residential addresses are public information. I did not purloin anyone's Rolodex to find these street locations. Every address in this book was obtained through access to public records that are open to every citizen. I simply did the legwork most people don't have time for. I spent close to a thousand hours rolling through microfilm records of real estate transactions. I pored over old City Directories from the days when even the upper crust would list their street addresses and phone numbers, and I worked with clerks at voter registration offices in two states and the District of Columbia. (Not that the common phone directory isn't sometimes useful. The very patrician J. Carter Brown, descendent of one of Rhode Island's first families and director emeritus of the National Gallery of Art, is listed, as is Austin Kiplinger of publishing fame.)

These addresses were then confirmed through a second source, often a neighbor or letter carrier who would be happy to point out, say, where Colin Powell lives. And speaking of General Powell—who at this writing has not declared whether he intends to run for president—these addresses are accurate as this guide goes to press, but a few might have changed in the several months between manuscript and publication. For people are mobile these days and change residences regularly.

Another occasional second source of an address is the social registries of metropolitan Washington. These registers are nicknamed the Blue Book and the Green Book, although their actual titles are *The Blue Book of Washington, D. C.* and *The Social List of Washington, D. C.* Each of these guides costs more than $100, although you can find them, as I did, in your public library.

It amuses me that bluebloods who will not list their names in any other directory—who, in fact, try to discourage us commoners from knowing where they live—will gladly put their names, addresses, phone numbers and information about their families in a guidebook just because inclusion in it carries social cachet.

For example, the Mars family, with a candy fortune worth $14 billion, is well known to be obsessively secretive. When I wrote their story in my recent book, *Crisis in Candyland: Melting the Chocolate Shell of the Mars Family Empire,* I detailed how Forrest

Mars Sr. would throw a napkin over his face when he saw a camera, to prevent his being photographed; that son Forrest Jr. travels under a pseudonym; and how daughter Jackie was furious when the family was listed in the Forbes 400 list of America's wealthiest families. Even the Mars corporate headquarters building in McLean is without a sign giving the company name.

Yet when I opened Washington's two social registers, there were the Marses, for anyone to see, listed with their home addresses, the locations of vacation homes, their children's names and where their children attended school. Apparently, folks of this statusphere believe that this information will be available only to others in their monied clique.

Celebrity Washington is intended to be both a resource for everyday people who want their letters to get to the person to whom they're sent and, more important, for those of us who like to take Sunday drives and ooh and aah at the houses and neighborhoods of the rich and famous.

Just as my family had the sense and good manners to keep on driving on those rare occasions when we saw a funeral service being conducted near a monument we wanted to examine close up, I remind the reader to observe rather than annoy, and to be cognizant that trespassing on private property is both bad form and in violation of local law.

Then, since Washington's gustatory pleasures are far more complex than the Good Humor treats of the 50s, after your Sunday outing you can refresh yourself at one of the restaurants cited in this guide, and spot even more celebrities while you relax.

Celebrity Washington's Quick Facts

• Established NEWSMEDIA STARS tend to cluster in Georgetown. Younger media types have not yet chosen a favorite neighborhood, but live all over town.

• CABINET MEMBERS are scattered, but like living Downtown and in the Palisades neighborhood.

• POLITICOS AND POWERBROKERS tend to group, not surprisingly, on Capitol Hill. They also live in Kalorama Heights, Downtown and Foggy Bottom. When they choose the suburbs, they prefer either McLean, Virginia or Bethesda, Maryland.

• Four CONGRESSMEN (Mark Sanford and Bob Inglis of South Carolina, Pete Hoekstra of Michigan and Jack Kingston of Georgia) sleep in their House of Representatives offices and walk to the building next door to shower in the House gym. These representatives, all freshman Republicans, apparently don't feel they can afford to rent even an efficiency apartment on their $134,000 salaries (plus $3,000 in tax deductions for living expenses).

• The WEALTHY usually stay in the city. They live in Georgetown, Kalorama Heights or Massachusetts Heights. Those who prefer the suburbs live in Potomac, Maryland.

• In the 60S AND 70S, Spring Valley and Wesley Heights were the preferred neighborhoods of the wealthy. Also, in the past, Arlington, Virginia spawned a number of children who grew up to be entertainers and media stars.

• Virtually all celebrities living in Foggy Bottom reside at the WATERGATE.

• GEORGETOWN ties with McLEAN, Virginia for the neighborhood with the most celebrities. Yet if you eliminate the clannish Kennedys, all of whom have houses or property in McLean, Georgetown comes in first in celebrity popularity.

MEDIA STARS

ANDERSON, JACK
7810 Kachina Lane, Potomac, MD 20854
One of the country's most widely read syndicated columnists and a Pulitzer prize winner who has been a thorn in the side of the Washington establishment for decades.

APPLE, R.W. "JOHNNY"
1509 28th St. NW, DC 20007 (Georgetown)
As Washington bureau chief of the *New York Times,* Johnny Apple is nearly as important in this town as his neighbor **KAY GRAHAM** (below). He also has a farm near Gettysburg.

BAKER, RUSSELL
202 West Market, Leesburg, VA 22075
New York Times syndicated columnist and author.

BALDRIGE, LETITIA
2339 Massachusetts Ave. NW, DC 20008 (Kalorama Heights)
Tish became the nation's foremost etiquette expert after leaving her post as White House social secretary to Jacqueline Bouvier Kennedy (see **KENNEDY, JACK/JACKIE** in PAST).

BLITZER, WOLF
8929 Holly Leaf Lane, Bethesda, MD 20817
White House correspondent for CNN.

BRADLEE, BEN/QUINN, SALLY
3014 N St. NW, DC 20007 (Georgetown)
Before retiring as *Washington Post* executive editor, Ben Bradlee was a newsman who served as a model for others. Sally Quinn is a novelist—*Happy Endings*—and occasional feature writer. Despite Ben's retirement, they are still at the top of Washington's social list.

BRINKLEY, DAVID
111 E. Melrose St., Chevy Chase, MD 20815
Retired NBC evening anchor and host of "This Week With David Brinkley."

BROCK, DAVID
3334 N St. NW, DC 20007 (Georgetown)
Journalist and author of best–selling investigative book *The Real Anita Hill*.

BRODER, DAVID
4024 27th St. N, Arlington VA 22207
Washington Post syndicated columnist and author.

BUCHANAN, PATRICK
1017 Savile Lane, McLean, VA 22101
Syndicated conservative columnist and GOP presidential primary candidate.

Pat Buchanan residence

BUCHWALD, ART
4327 Hawthorne St. NW, DC 20016 (Wesley Heights)
Humorist and syndicated columnist. Has summer place in Vineyard Haven at Martha's Vineyard.

BUCKLEY, CHRIS
3516 Newark St. NW, DC 20008 (Cleveland Park)
Son of Bill and Pat, editor of *Forbes FYI* and author.

DE BORCHGRAVE, ARNAUD
#32, 2141 Wyoming Ave. NW, DC 20008 (Kalorama Heights)
Former editor–in–chief of the *Washington Times* and chief of correspondents for *Newsweek*. Also has house in Palm Beach, FL.

DONALDSON, SAM
1125 Crest Lane, McLean, VA 22101
ABC News wiseguy.

DOWNEY, EDWARD M.
9010 Congressional Pkwy., Potomac, MD 20854
Publisher of *Military Life*.

DOWNIE, LEONARD
2932 Albermarle St. NW, DC 20008 (Forest Hills)
Washington Post editor whose wife, Geraldine Rebach, works from the house as a massage therapist.

EVANS, ROWLAND
3125 O St. NW, DC 20007 (Georgetown)
Syndicated columnist and television commentator.

FRIEDAN, BETTY
The Lansburgh, 425 8th St. NW, DC 20004 (Downtown)
Author of classic book *The Feminine Mystique* and social commentator.

GRAHAM, DONALD E.
3110 Newark St. NW, DC 20008 (Cleveland Park)
Current chairman of Washington Post Company, since mother Katharine's retirement. Empire also includes television and cable stations.

GRAHAM, KATHARINE
2920 R St. NW, DC 20007 (Georgetown)
Former chairman of Washington Post Company, including the *Washington Post* and *Newsweek;* heroine of Watergate in 1971–72. Has oceanfront house at Martha's Vineyard.

GROSVENOR, GILBERT M.
1312 Merchant Ln., McLean, VA 22101
President and heir to National Geographic Society.

HERSH, SEYMOUR
3214 Newark St., DC 20008 (Cleveland Park)
Freelance journalist, Pulitzer prize winner and author.

HITCHENS, CHRISTOPHER
The Wyoming, 2022 Columbia Road NW, DC 20009 (Adams–Morgan)
Washington columnist for *Vanity Fair* who keeps a smoke–filled apartment.

HUFFINGTON, ARIANNA S./MICHAEL
3005 45th St. NW, DC 20016 (Wesley Heights)
Arianna is an author, chairman of the Center for Effective Compassion at the Progress and Freedom Foundation, and the woman behind Michael, who recently lost the US Senate race and formerly was a US Representative (R) from California.

HUGHES, CATHY (CATHERINE L.)
6437 14th St. NW, DC 20012 (Brightwood)
Radio host and head of Radio One, Inc. which owns WOL–AM and WKYS–FM in the District, and WMMJ–FM in Bethesda.

HUME, BRIT
Apt. 9, 3100 N St. NW, DC 20007 (Georgetown)
CNN reporter, author and syndicated columnist for Washington Post Group.

KELLEY, KITTY
3037 Dumbarton Ave. NW, DC 20007 (Georgetown)
Author of best–selling, tell–all biographies of Nancy Reagan, Frank Sinatra and *Jackie–Oh!*

KESSLER, RON/PAMELA
2516 Stratton Dr., Potomac, MD 20854
Ron is bestselling author *(Inside the White House)*, former award-winning *Washington Post* reporter; Pamela is also a former *Post* writer and author of *Undercover Washington*.

KING, LARRY
Prospect House #855, 1200 N. Nash St., Arlington, VA 22209
Host of CNN "Larry King Live" and columnist.

Michael Kinsley residence

KINSLEY, MICHAEL
6908 Ridgewood Ave., Chevy Chase, MD 20815
CNN "Crossfire" host and columnist.

KIPLINGER, AUSTIN
Montevideo, 16801 River Rd., Poolesville, MD 20837
Owner and publisher of Kiplinger Washington Editors newsletters and books.

KOPPEL, TED
11910 Glenn Mill Rd., Potomac, MD 20854
Host of ABC "Nightline."

KRISTOL, IRVING
Watergate East #1104, 2510 Virginia Ave. NW, DC 20037 (Foggy Bottom)
Editor of *The Public Interest* and think–tank brain. Also father of **BILL KRISTOL,** GOP strategist and editor of *The Standard* (see POLITICOS).

LEHRER, JIM
3556 Macomb St. NW, DC 20016 (Cleveland Park)
Anchor of PBS "Lehrer NewsHour."

LEWIS, DELANO
12620 Travilah Rd., Potomac, MD 20854
CEO and president of National Public Radio.

LIMPERT, JACK (JOHN A.)
5300 Elliott Rd., Bethesda, MD 20816
Editor of *Washingtonian*.

MANKIEWICZ, FRANK
The Wyoming, Columbia Rd. NW, DC 20009 (Adams–Morgan)
NPR commentator, lobbyist and journalist. Former press secretary to RFK (see **KENNEDY, ETHEL** in PAST) during presidential primary.

MATTHEWS, CHRIS/KATHLEEN
3309 Quesada St. NW, DC 20015 (Chevy Chase)
Chris is a journalist and author. Kathleen is host of ABC's syndicated television show "Working Woman" and host of WJLA evening news.

MCCLENDON, SARAH
Kennedy–Warren, 3133 Connecticut Ave. NW, DC 20008 (Woodley Park)
Senior White House correspondent.

MERRILL, PHILIP
Watergate East, 2500 Virginia Ave. NW, DC 20037 (Foggy Bottom)
Owner of Capital Gazette News and chairman and publisher of *Washingtonian* and *Baltimore* magazines.

MITCHELL, ANDREA
2710 Chain Bridge Rd. NW, DC 20016 (Palisades)
NBC News White House correspondent.

O'ROURKE, P.J.
Kennedy–Warren, 3133 Connecticut Ave. NW, DC 20008 (Woodley Park)
Political author—*Parliament of Whores*—and *Rolling Stone* feature writer.

ORTH, MAUREEN/RUSSERT, TIM
3124 Woodley Rd. NW, DC 20008 (Cleveland Park)
She is a feature writer for *Vanity Fair* and other magazines. He is NBC bureau chief and news anchor.

PETERSON, GORDON
3700 Blackthorn Ct., Chevy Chase, MD 20815
Familiar WUSA local news anchor (channel 9).

POVICH, SHIRLEY
Colonnade, 2801 New Mexico Ave. NW, DC 20007 (Wesley Heights)
Veteran sports writer with a 72-year career and father of television's Maury.

QUINN, SALLY see BRADLEE, BEN

RASKIN, BARBARA
1820 Wyoming Ave. NW, DC 20008 (Kalorama Heights)
Best-selling novelist of *Hot Flashes,* among other books.

REGARDIE, BILL
2319 Bancroft Pl. NW, DC 20008 (Kalorama Heights)
Publisher of the on-again, off-again eponymous business magazine and of *New Homes Guide.*

ROBERTS, STEVE/COKIE
5315 Bradley Blvd., Bethesda, MD 20814
He is senior writer at *U.S. News and World Report.* She is a panelist on ABC "This Week With David Brinkley" and NPR "Morning Edition." This is the house Cokie grew up in with brother **TOM BOGGS** and later bought from her mother **LINDY BOGGS** (see POLITICOS).

ROWAN, CARL
3116 Fessenden St. NW, DC 20008 (Forest Hills)
Syndicated *Washington Post* columnist. Warning: Do not approach backyard Jacuzzi.

RUSSERT, TIM see ORTH, MAUREEN

SAFIRE, WILLIAM
6200 Elmwood Rd., Chevy Chase, MD 20815
New York Times columnist and word maven; conservative politico and speechwriter.

SALINGER, PIERRE
3114 O St. NW, DC 20007 (Georgetown)
Formerly **JFK** (see PAST) press secretary; now PR honcho.

SCHIEFFER, BOB
2438 Belmont Rd. NW, DC 20008 (Kalorama Heights)
CBS News anchor and moderator, "Face the Nation."

SCHORR, DANIEL
3113 Woodley Rd. NW, DC 20008-3491 (Cleveland Park)
Former CBS and CNN news correspondant, now National Public Radio commentator who gets so much mail that he has requested his own four-digit delivery sector zip code from the Post Office.

SESNO, FRANK
11104 Burywood Ln., Reston, VA 22094
CNN anchor.

SHALES, TOM
1650 Kirby Rd., McLean, VA 22101
Nationally esteemed television critic for the *Washington Post*.

SHAW, BERNARD
7526 Heatherton Ln., Potomac, MD 20854
CNN anchor.

THOMAS, HELEN
Shoreham North Apt., 2501 Calvert St. NW, DC 20008 (Woodley Park)
Senior White House correspondent for UPI.

THOMPSON, LEE
9000 Belmart Rd., Potomac, MD 20854
Host of television special reports.

TOTENBERG, NINA/HASKELL, FLOYD
133 N. Carolina Ave. SE, DC 20003 (Capitol Hill)
She is NPR host, CNN "Crossfire" member and the woman who put Anita Hill in the news; he is former US Senator (D) from Colorado.

Nina Totenberg/Floyd Haskell residence

VALENTI, JACK
4635 Ashby St. NW, DC 20007 (Foxhall)
President of Motion Picture Association of America, often a speaker at the televised Oscar awards presentation.

VANCE, JIM
4125 52nd St. NW, DC 20016 (Spring Valley)
WRC television newscaster.

WERTHEIMER, FRED/LINDA
3502 Macomb St. NW, DC 20007 (Cleveland Park)
She is host of NPR "All Things Considered"; he is former Common Cause president.

WILL, GEORGE
9 Grafton St., Chevy Chase, MD 20815
Conservative *Washington Post* columnist who is syndicated to 475 papers.

WOODWARD, BOB/WALSH, ELSA
2907 Q St. NW, DC 20007 (Georgetown)
He is the well–known Watergate sleuth and author; she is author of *Divided Lives*. Besides this 1868 house, they own a place on Chesapeake Bay near Annapolis.

WOUK, HERMAN
3255 N St. NW, DC 20007 (Georgetown)
Best–selling author for nearly 50 years—*Caine Mutiny, Marjorie Morningstar, Youngblood Hawke*. Recent book is *The Glory*.

Clinton's Crowd

ALBRIGHT, MADELINE
1318 34th St. NW, DC 20007 (Georgetown)
Chief US delegate to the United Nations.

The Lansburgh—Jane Alexander and Janet Reno residence

ALEXANDER, JANE
The Lansburgh, 425 8th St. NW, DC 20004 (Downtown)
Chairman of the National Endowment for the Arts and actor.

BABBITT, BRUCE
5169 Watson St. NW, DC 20016 (Palisades)
US Secretary of the Interior.

BILLINGTON, JAMES
1520 Highwood Dr., McLean, Va 22101
US Librarian of Congress.

BROWN, RON
2722 Unicorn Ln. NW, DC 20015 (Barnaby Woods)
US Secretary of Commerce.

CISNEROS, HENRY
5026 Reno Rd. NW, DC 20008 (Chevy Chase)
US Secretary of Housing and Urban Development.

CUOMO, ANDREW/KERRY KENNEDY
1344 Richland Ter., McLean, VA 22101
Andrew is Deputy Secretary of HUD and son of former NY Governor Cuomo; Kerry is Bobby and Ethel's daughter (see **KENNEDY, ETHEL** in PAST) who co–chairs Amnesty International Leadership Council.

DUFFEY, JOSEPH
5058 Lowell St., DC 20016 (Palisades)
Director of US Information Agency.

GLICKMAN, DAN
4442 Hawthorne St. NW, DC 20016 (Wesley Heights)
US Secretary of Agriculture.

HARRIMAN, PAMELA
3038 N St. NW, DC 20007 (Georgetown)
US Ambassador to France. House with formal gardens, pool and four–car parking is for sale at $3.3 million, as is the 60–acre estate, Willow Oaks, near Middleburg that Madame Ambassador inherited from late husband Averell. Also has estates in Sun Valley, Idaho and Arden, New York. This house's adjacent 1892 building, formerly used by the Harrimans as office space and to host out–of–town guests, sold recently for $990,000 as compared to a list price of $1.5 million.

KANTOR, MICKEY
5019 Klingle St. NW, DC 20016 (Palisades)
US Trade representative.

KENDALL, DAVID
5215 Massachusetts Ave., Bethesda, MD 20816
President Clinton's personal attorney.

LAKE, ANTHONY
4701 45th St. NW, DC 20016 (American
    University Park)
National Security Advisor.

Anthony Lake residence

O'LEARY, HAZEL
Somerset House, 5600 Wisconsin Ave., Chevy Chase, MD 20815
US Secretary of Energy.

PENA, FEDERICO
3517 Sterling Ave., Alexandria, VA 22304
US Secretary of Transportation.

PERRY, WILLIAM J.
8017 Rising Ridge Rd., Bethesda, MD 20817
US Secretary of Defense.

RENO, JANET
The Lansburgh, 425 8th St. NW, DC 20004 (Downtown)
US Attorney General. Also residing at the Lansburgh is Rep. **JOE KENNEDY JR.** Also, **PRESIDENT ARISTIDE** of Haiti keeps an apartment here (see POLITICOS).

RILEY, RICHARD
The Broadmoor, 3601 Connecticut Ave. NW, DC 20008 (Cleveland
    Park)
US Secretary of Education. **RICHARD NIXON** (see PAST) lived in this apartment house when he was a congressman from California.

RIVLIN, ALICE
2838 Chesterfield Pl. NW, DC 20008 (Forest Hills)
Head of US Office of Management and Budget.

RUBIN, BOB
Jefferson Hotel, 1200 16th St.
NW, DC 20036
(Downtown)
US Secretary of the Treasury and richest member of Clinton administration. Earned $26.5 million as co-chair of investment giant Goldman Sachs & Co. in 1992 and can afford a permanent suite at this hotel.

Jefferson Hotel—Bob Rubin residence

SHALALA, DONNA
3551 Winfield Ln. NW, DC 20007 (Georgetown)
US Secretary of Health and Human Services.

STEPHANOPOULOS, GEORGE
Lives above Eye Gottcha store, 1511 Connecticut Ave. NW, DC 20036 (Dupont Circle)
Adviser to President Clinton.

TALBOTT, STROBE
2812 Calvert St. NW, DC 20008 (Woodley Park)
US Deputy Secretary of State.

POLITICOS AND POWERBROKERS

AKAKA, DANIEL
3656 Gunston Rd., Alexandria, VA 22302
US Senator (D) from Hawaii.

ALTMAN, ROBERT/CARTER, LINDA
9200 Harrington Dr., Potomac, MD 20854
Altman is an attorney who was acquitted in BCCI charges and is a Democratic insider. Carter was television's "Wonder Woman."

ARISTIDE, JEAN-BERTRAND
The Lansburgh, 425 8th St. NW, DC 20004 (Downtown)
When away from Haiti, President Aristide resides in the same building as Attorney General **JANET RENO** (see CLINTON'S CROWD) and Rep. **JOE KENNEDY JR.** (below).

BAKER, HOWARD
Market Square, 801 Pennsylvania Ave. NW, DC 20004 (Downtown)
Former US Senator (R) from Tennessee and chief of staff in White House to Ronald Reagan. Combined three condos into one gorgeous living space. Also has house in Huntsville, TN.

BARRY, MARION
161 Raleigh St. SE, DC 20032 (Congress Heights)
DC mayor. Electronic and other security for this house cost nearly $100,000. Take a look at the shed that cost $38,000.

BENNETT, BILL
20 W. Lenox St., Chevy Chase, MD 20815
Conservative writer, former US drug czar and US Education Secretary.

BENNETT, BOB
665 Potomac River Rd., McLean, VA 22102
Powerful lawyer and brother of **BILL BENNETT** (above).

BENTSEN, LLOYD
1810 Kalorama Sq. NW, DC 20008 (Kalorama Heights)
Former US Treasury secretary under Clinton and former US Senator (D) from Texas. Now with area law firm.

BINGAMAN, JEFF
5028 Overlook Rd. NW, DC 20016 (Spring Valley)
US Senator (D) from New Mexico.

BOGGS, LINDY
2029 Connecticut Ave. NW, DC 20008 (Kalorama Heights)
US Representative from Louisiana, 1973 to 1990. Still maintains residence in DC. Mother of **TOM** (below), and **COKIE ROBERTS** (see MEDIA).

BOGGS, THOMAS
6 E Kirk St., Chevy Chase, MD 20815
Both of Tommy Boggs' parents were US congressional representatives. He is DC's most influential lobbyist.

BOND, CHRISTOPHER (KIT)
4859 Rockwood Pkwy. NW, DC 20016 (Spring Valley)
US Senator (R) from Missouri.

BONO, SONNY
3934 Highwood Ct. NW, DC 20007 (Georgetown)
US Representative (R) from California, former singer and Cher spouse.

BOREN, DAVID
2369 S. Queen St., Arlington, VA 22202
Former US Senator (D) from Oklahoma.

BRADLEY, BILL
3461 Macomb St. NW, DC 20016 (Cleveland Park)
US Senator (D) from New Jersey.

BREAUX, JOHN
114 5th St. NE, DC 20002 (Capitol Hill)
US Senator (D) from Louisiana.

BRIMMER, ANDREW F.
4910 32nd St. NW, DC 20008 (Forest Hills)
Appointed by US Congress to head Washington DC's financial control board. Formerly governor of Federal Reserve Board, also heads financial consulting firm Brimmer and Company, Inc.

BUMPERS, DALE
7613 Honesty Way, Bethesda, MD 20817
US Senator (D) from Arkansas.

CACHERIS, PLATO
1319 Bishop Ln., Alexandria, VA 22302
Attorney for **JACK KENT COOKE** (see SUPERRICH) and Fawn Hall. Recent client is counterspy **ALDRICH AMES** (see PAST).

CAMPBELL, BEN NIGHTHORSE
456 New Jersey Ave. SE, DC 20003 (Capitol Hill)
US Senator (R) from Colorado; the only Native American in Senate.

CARLUCCI, FRANK
1207 Crest Ln., McLean, VA 22101
Chairman of The Carlyle Group; former US Secretary of Defense.

CHAFEE, JOHN
7110 Thrasher Rd., McLean, VA 22101
US Senator (R) from Rhode Island.

CHENEY, RICHARD/LYNNE
6613 Madison Dr., McLean, VA 22101
Under George Bush's administration, Dick was US Defense secretary and Lynne headed National Endowment for the Arts.

CLIFFORD, CLARK
9421 Rockville Pike, Bethesda, MD 20814
Democratic kingmaker until BCCI scandal. Also has summer home in Nantucket, MA.

CLINGER, WILLIAM F. JR.
418 St. Asaph St., Alexandria, VA 22314
US Representative (R) from Pennsylvania who heads House Government Reform and Oversight Committee.

COCHRAN, THAD
6213 Foxcroft Rd., Alexandria, VA 22307
US Senator (R) from Mississippi.

COVERDELL, PAUL
601 Pennsylvania Ave. NW, DC 20004 (Downtown)
US Senator (R) from Georgia. Fellow congressman **BOB TORRICELLI** (below) also lives in this building.

CUTLER, LLOYD/KRAFT, POLLY
3115 O St. NW, DC 20007 (Georgetown)
He's served as attorney for the last two Democratic presidents; she's an artist.

DANFORTH, JOHN
5101 Van Ness St. NW, DC 20016 (Spring Valley)
Former US Senator (R) from Missouri.

DECONCINI, DENNIS
6014 Chesterbrook Rd., McLean, VA 22101
Former US Senator (D) from Arizona.

DELLUMS, RONALD
5423 28th St. NW, DC 20015 (Chevy Chase)
Former US Representative (D) from California.

DOLE, ROBERT/ELIZABETH
Watergate South, 700 New Hampshire Ave. NW, DC 20037 (Foggy Bottom)
Bob is US Senator (R) from Kanasas and Senate Minority Leader, as well as perennial presidential primary candidate. Libby now heads the American Red Cross and was US Secretary of Housing and Urban Development under George Bush.

DOMENICI, PETE
120 3rd St. NE, DC 20002 (Capitol Hill)
Former US Senator (R) from New Mexico.

DORGAN, BYRON
1702 Esquire Ln., McLean, VA 22101
US Senator (D) from North Dakota.

EDELMAN, MARIAN WRIGHT
3208 Newark St. NW; DC 20008 (Cleveland Park)
Head of Children's Defense Fund and friend of Hillary.

EDWARDS, DON
Watergate West, 2700 Virginia Ave. NW, DC 20037 (Foggy Bottom)
Former US Representative (D) from California.

EXON, J. JAMES
4920 Sentinel Dr., Bethesda, MD 20816
US Senator (D) from Nebraska.

FEINSTEIN, DIANNE
#4, 1825 Kalorama Sq., DC 20008 (Kalorama Heights)
US Senator (D) from California.

FOLEY, MARK
Watergate, 700 New Hampshire Ave. NW, DC 20037 (Foggy Bottom)
US Representative (R) from Florida.

FOLEY, TOM
2219 California St. NW, DC 20008 (Kalorama Heights)
Lobbyist, former Speaker of the House (D).

FORD, WENDELL
4974 Sentinel Dr., Bethesda, MD 20816
US Senator (D) from Kentucky.

FRIST, BILL
2860 Woodland Dr. NW, DC 20008 (Massachusetts Heights)
US Senator (R) from Tennessee.

GEPHARDT, RICHARD
9203 White Chimney Ln., Great Falls, VA 22066
US Representative (D) from St. Louis, MO and former Majority Leader of House; sometime presidential candidate.

GERGEN, DAVID
1105 Alvord Ct., McLean, VA 22102
Republican who became Bill Clinton's presidential counselor.

Gingrich, Gore, Heflin residence

GINGRICH, NEWT
110 Maryland Ave. NE, DC 20002 (Capitol Hill)
US Representative (R) from Georgia and Speaker of the House.

GINSBURG, RUTH BADER
Watergate South, 700 New Hampshire Ave. NW, DC 20037 (Foggy Bottom)
Associate Justice, US Supreme Court.

GONZALEZ, HENRY
110 D St. SE, DC 20003 (Capitol Hill)
US Representative (D) from Texas.

GORE, AL SR.
110 Maryland Ave. NE, DC 20002 (Capitol Hill)
Father of Vice President and former US Senator (D) from Tennessee. Keeps this apartment for his DC visits. Neighbor of **NEWT GINGRICH** (above) and **HOWELL HEFLIN** (below).

GORTON, SLADE
408 A St. NE, DC 20002 (Capitol Hill)
US Senator (R) from Washington.

GRAMM, PHIL/WENDY
4201 Yuma St. NW, DC 20016 (Tenley)
He is US Senator (R) from Texas; she is influential economist.

GREENSPAN, ALAN
Watergate, 700 New Hampshire Ave. NW DC 20037 (Foggy Bottom)
Chairman of the Federal Reserve Board.

HASKELL, FLOYD see TOTENBERG, NINA (MEDIA)

HATCH, ORRIN
2127 Galloping Way, Vienna, VA 22181
US Senator (R) from Utah.

HEFLIN, HOWELL
110 Maryland Ave. NE, DC 20002 (Capitol Hill)
US Senator (D) from Alabama, lives in same building as **GINGRICH** and **GORE** (above).

HELMS, JESSE
2820 S. Joyce St., Arlington, VA 22202
US Senator (R) from North Carolina.

HOLLINGS, ERNEST
3846 Macomb St. NW, DC 20016 (Cleveland Park)
US Senator (D) from South Carolina.

HOUGHTON, AMORY, JR.
3512 P St. NW, DC 20007 (Georgetown)
US Representative (R) from New York. Descendent of founder of Corning Glass; owns seven percent of stock.

HOYER, STENY
6621 Lacona St., District Heights, MD 20747
US Representative (D) from Prince George's Co., Maryland.

HUFFINGTON, MICHAEL see HUFFINGTON, ARIANNA (MEDIA)

INOUYE, DANIEL
8013 Herb Farm Dr., Bethesda, MD 20817
US Senator (D) from Hawaii.

JACKSON, JESSE
400 T St. NW, DC 20001 (Ledroit Park)
African–American leader and presidential primary candidate.

JARVIS, CHARLENE DREW
1789 Sycamore St. NW, DC 20012 (Colonial Village)
DC Council member.

JEFFORDS, JAMES
533 7th St. SE, DC 20003 (Capitol Hill)
US Senator (R) from Vermont.

JOHNSTON, J. BENNETT JR.
1317 Merrie Ridge Rd., McLean, VA 22101
US Senator (D) from Louisiana.

JORDAN, VERNON E. JR.
4610 Kenmore Dr. NW, DC 20007 (Fox Hall Village)
Friend Of Bill, attorney and former president of Urban League. Keeps fashionable summer digs at Martha's Vineyard's Chilmark.

KAMBER, VIC
129 11th St. NE, DC 20002 (Capitol Hill)
Democratic fundraiser and strategist.

KASSEBAUM, NANCY
2408 California St. NW, DC 20008 (Kalorama Heights)
US Senator (R) from Kansas.

KELLY, SHARON PRATT
1525 Iris St. NW, DC 20012 (Colonial Village)
Former DC mayor.

KEMP, JACK
7904 Greentree Rd., Bethesda, MD 20817
Former US Representative (R) from NY and former Housing and Urban Development secretary under George Bush.

KENNEDY, ANTHONY
6819 Wemberly Way, McLean, VA 22101
Associate Justice, US Supreme Court. Lives on same street as fellow Associate Justice **ANTONIN SCALIA,** below.

Anthony Kennedy residence

KENNEDY, JOSEPH P. JR.
The Lansburg, 425 8th St. NW, DC 20004 (Downtown)
US Representative (D) from Massachusetts; owns, with Uncle **TED KENNEDY** (below), empty lot on Chain Bridge Rd., McLean, VA. Lot, with Potomac River view, valued at $960,000.

KENNEDY, TED
636 Chain Bridge Rd., McLean, VA 22101
US Senator (D) from Massachusetts, brother of **JFK** and **RFK** (see PAST).

KRAFT, POLLY see CUTLER, LLOYD

KRISTOL, WILLIAM
6800 Baron Rd., McLean, VA 22101
GOP strategist who was Vice President Dan Quayle's chief of staff. Now editor/publisher of Rupert Murdoch's new conservative weekly *The Standard*. Son of **IRVING** (see MEDIA).

LAMB, BRIAN P.
2420 S. Queen St., Arlington, VA 22202
Chairman, C–Span.

LAPIERRE, WAYNE R.
9620 Masterworks Dr., Vienna, VA 22181
Heads the National Rifle Association.

LEACH, JIM
2124 Kalorama Rd. NW, DC 20008 (Kalorama Heights)
US Representative (R) from Iowa who heads the House Banking Committee.

LEVIN, CARL
1017 East Capitol St. SE, DC 20003 (Capitol Hill)
US Senator (D) from Michigan.

LOTT, TRENT
509 Third St. SE, DC 20003 (Capitol Hill)
US Senator from Mississippi.

LUGAR, RICHARD
7841 Old Dominion Dr., McLean, VA 22101
US Senator (R) from Indiana.

Carl Levin residence

MCCAIN, JOHN
1300 Crystal Dr., Arlington, VA 22202
US Senator (R) from Arizona.

METZENBAUM, HOWARD
4512 Foxhall Crescent NW, DC 20007 (Foxhall)
Former US Senator (D) from Ohio.

MEYERS, JAN
1805 Crystal Dr., Arlington, VA 22202
US Representative (D) from Kansas who heads House Small Business Committee.

MICHEL, ROBERT H.
320 8th St. SE, DC 20003 (Capitol Hill)
US Representative (R) from Illinois.

MORELLA, CONNIE/TONY
6601 Millwood Rd., Bethesda, MD 20817
Connie is the US Representative (R) from suburban Maryland and Tony is an attorney and partner, Hewes, Morella, Gelband & Lamberton.

MOYNIHAN, (DANIEL) PATRICK
Market Square Apts., #111, 801 Pennsylvania Ave. NW, DC 20004 (Downtown)
US Senator (D) from New York.

NICKLES, DON
9118 Cricklewood Ct., Vienna, VA 22180
US Senator (R) from Oklahoma.

NORTON, ELEANOR HOLMES
10 9th St. SE, DC 20003 (Capitol Hill)
DC delegate (D) to US Congress.

Eleanor Holmes Norton Residence

NUNN, SAM
6852 Tulip Hill Terrace, Bethesda, MD 20816
US Senator (D) from Georgia.

OBERSTAR, JAMES
10014 Carter Rd., Bethesda, MD 20817
US Representative (D) from Minnesota.

OBEY, DAVID
3920 N. 36th St., Arlington, VA 22207
US Representative (D) from Wisconsin.

PELL, CLAIBORNE
3425 Prospect St. NW, DC 20007 (Georgetown)
Very wealthy blueblood US Senator (D) from Rhode Island. House was built in 1798.

PERCY, CHARLES (CHUCK)
1691 34th St. NW, DC 20007 (Georgetown)
Lobbyist and former US Senator (R) from Illinois.

POWELL, COLIN
1317 Ballantrae Farm Dr., McLean, VA 22101
Former Chairman US Joint Chiefs of Staff.

PRESSLER, LARRY
115 4th St. SE, DC 20003 (Capitol Hill)
US Senator from North Dakota (R) who heads Commerce Committee.

PRYOR, DAVID
1615 19th St., DC 20009 (Dupont Circle)
US Senator (D) from Arkansas.

RANGEL, CHARLES
4807 Colorado Ave., DC 20011 (Crestwood)
US Representative (D) from New York.

RAY, JOHN
4310 20th St. NE, DC 20018 (Lamond Riggs)
DC Council member (D).

REHNQUIST, WILLIAM
2329 N. Glebe Rd., Arlington, VA 22207
Chief Justice of the United States, US Supreme Court.

REID, HARRY
1326 Kirby Rd., McLean, VA 22101
US Senator (D) from Nevada.

ROBB, CHUCK/LYNDA
612 Chain Bridge Rd., McLean, VA 22101
Chuck is US Senator (D) from Virginia; Lynda is **LBJ** daughter (see PAST).

ROBERTS, PAT
2203 White Oaks Dr., Alexandria, VA 22306
US Representative from Kansas (R) who heads House Agriculture Committee.

ROCKEFELLER, JAY (JOHN D. IV)/SHARON PERCY
1940 Shepherd St. NW, DC 20011 (Crestwood)
Jay is very wealthy US Senator (D) from West Virginia. Sharon is former head of WETA and daughter of former US Senator from Illinois, **CHARLES PERCY,** above. House cost $6.5 million and Jay put an additional $8 million into renovation and refurbishment.

SASSER, JAMES
4810 32nd St. NW, DC 20008 (Chevy Chase)
Former US Senator (D) from Tennessee.

SCALIA, ANTONIN
6713 Wemberly Way, McLean, VA 22101
Associate Justice, US Supreme Court.

SCHROEDER, PATRICIA
4102 Lester Ct., Alexandria, VA 22311
US Representative (D) from Colorado.

SHRIVER, MARK K.
10014 Carter Rd., Bethesda, MD 20817
His last name comes from father **SARGE SHRIVER** (see Past) and the K. stands for Kennedy, his mother's side of the family. Mark is Maryland's new state delegate and an up–and–coming Democratic power.

SIMON, PAUL
510 N St. SW, DC 20024 (Waterfront)
US Senator (D) from Illinois.

SIMPSON, ALAN
1112 Brentfield Dr., McLean, VA 22101
US Senator (R) from Wyoming.

SNOWE, OLYMPIA
216 Justice Ct. NE, DC 20002 (Capitol Hill)
US Senator (R) from Maine.

STENHOLM, CHARLES
4710 N. 40th St., Arlington, VA 22207
US Representative (D) from Texas.

Paul Simon residence

STEVENS, JOHN PAUL
1101 S. Arlington Ridge Rd., Arlington, VA 22202
Associate Justice, US Supreme Court.

STRAUSS, ROBERT
Watergate East, 2500 Virginia Ave. NW, DC 20037 (Foggy Bottom)
Democratic adviser and former head of Democratic National Committee, former ambassador to USSR.

SULLIVAN, BRENDAN V. JR.
4926 Rockwood Parkway NW, DC 20016 (Spring Valley)
High-powered lawyer who represented Ollie North during the US Senate Iran-contra hearings. Bristling, he told the senators who, he felt, ignored him that he was not a "potted plant."

THOMPSON, FRED
701 Pennsylvania Ave. NW, DC 20004 (Downtown)
US Senator (R) from Tennessee and movie/TV actor.

TORRICELLI, BOB
601 Pennsylvania Ave. NW, DC 20004 (Downtown)
Representative (D) from New Jersey. Neighbor of US Senator **PAUL COVERDELL** (above).

TRACHTENBERG, STEVE
2241 Bancroft Pl. NW, Kalorama Heights, DC 20008 (Kalorama Heights)
President of George Washington University.

WALLOP, MALCOLM
4834 Van Ness St. NW, DC 20016 (Spring Valley)
Former US Senator (R) from Wyoming and now head of the think tank Frontiers of Freedom.

WARNER, JOHN
Watergate, 700 New Hampshire Ave. NW, DC 20037 (Foggy Bottom)
US Senator (R) from Virginia.

WAXMAN, HENRY
6913 Ayr Ln., Bethesda, MD 20817
US Representative (D) from California.

WEINBERGER, CASPAR
Watergate, 700 New Hampshire Ave. NW, DC 20037 (Foggy Bottom)
Business leader, former US Secretary of Defense. Also has home in Maine.

WOLFENSOHN, JAMES
Kalorama Circle, DC 20008 (Kalorama Heights)
World Bank president, former Kennedy Center chairman. House includes a four-car garage.

YOUNG, DON
9504 Brian Jac Lane, Great Falls, VA 22066
US Representative from Alaska (R) who heads House Public Lands and Resources Committee.

SuperRich, Athletes & Entertainers

ALLBRITTON, JOSEPH
2940 Foxhall Rd. NW, DC 20016 (Wesley Heights)
Chairman and part–owner of Riggs Bank, where Abraham Lincoln had an account. Founded Allbritton Communications, a conglomerate of television stations including WJLA (channel 7) and Newschannel 8.

BAINUM, STEWART JR.
12 Primrose St., Chevy Chase, MD 20815
Multi–millionaire businessman, heir to Manor Care, Inc., a national chain of nursing homes. Also a franchiser of motels and hotels, including Quality Inn. Mentioned as a possible MD gubernatorial candidate.

BINGHAM, JOAN
1321 31st St. NW, DC 20007 (Georgetown)
Member of feuding newspaper family that owned the Louisville *Courier–Journal*. Inherited about $40 million and got millions more when the paper was sold for $435 million.

BROWN, J. CARTER
3035 Dumbarton Ave. NW, DC 20007 (Georgetown)
Director emeritus of National Gallery of Art, descendent of family that founded Brown University.

BRUCE, EVANGELINE
1405 34th St. NW, DC 20007 (Georgetown)
Widow of David Bruce, diplomatic US triple–crown ambassador (to Great Britain, France and Germany). After their daughter's murder, Evangeline founded Sasha Bruce Youthwork to help troubled young people. Also author of recent book *Napoleon & Josephine*.

CAFRITZ, CALVIN
1642 29th St. NW, DC 20007 (Georgetown)
Heir to Cafritz Co., a real estate developer that also owns commercial and residential space, privately held. Calvin worked for the family foundation, now is on his own.

CAFRITZ, CARTER
4340 Cathedral Ave. NW, DC 20016 (Wesley Heights)
Also a real estate heir but runs his own eponymous company.

CAFRITZ, CONRAD/PEGGY
3030 Chain Bridge Rd. NW, DC 20016 (Palisades)
Fought with brother over mother's estate. Has developed a dozen residential hotels in Washington.

CARR, OLIVER T.
6037 Ridge Rd., Bethesda, MD 20817
CEO Oliver Carr Co., a commercial developer that built a good deal of downtown Washington. The land this house is on is estimated at $2.5 million.

CARR, ROBERT O.
5019 Sedgwick St. NW, DC 20016 (Spring Valley)
Heir to Oliver Carr Co., a diversified real estate development company that is privately owned.

CARTER, LINDA see ALTMAN, ROBERT (POLITICOS)

CASSERLY, CHARLEY
15 Moss Rd., Sterling, VA 20165
Redskins general manager.

COOKE, JACK KENT
2801 Rock Creek Dr. NW, DC 20008 (Massachusetts Heights)
Billionaire media baron *(Los Angeles Daily News)* and Redskins owner has put this house up for sale but he won't be homeless. He also has estate, "Far Acres," near Middleburg.

COYNE, MARSHALL
2230 S. St. NW, DC 20008 (Kalorama Heights)
Chairman of the board of the Madison Hotel. Paid $2 million for this Georgian house with double drawing rooms and pool.

DAVIS, EVELYN Y.
Watergate East, 2500 Virginia Ave., DC 20037 (Foggy Bottom)
"Gadfly" who attends annual meetings and makes free–spending corporate executives wish they worked for privately owned businesses.

DELL, DONALD L.
12200 Stoney Creek Rd., Potomac, MD 20854
Past tennis champion and owner of ProServ has a 45–acre spread on which to chase tennis balls.

DIKEMBE, MUTOMBO
11513 Lake Potomac Dr., Potomac, MD 20854
Georgetown graduate who signed with the Denver Nuggets.

EWING, PATRICK
9712 Sorrell Ave., Potomac, MD 20854
Former Hoya who now plays for New York Knicks.

FELD, KENNETH
9609 Halter Ct., Potomac, MD 20854
Ringling Bros. and Barnum & Bailey heir.

GREEN, DARRELL
21321 Comus Ct., Ashburn, VA 22011
Redskin cornerback.

HAFT, GLORIA and LINDA
8709 Burning Tree Rd., Bethesda, MD 20817
Linda is estranged from father **HERBERT** (below); mother Gloria bought house from daughter although Linda still uses this address as her legal residence.

HAFT, HERBERT
2501 30th St. NW, DC 20008 (Kalorama Heights)
Current Chairman, Dart Group. Paid $1.7 million for lot and house, then razed the stately mansion to build current residence, costing an additional $4.5 million. **GLORIA** filed a notice of foreclosure to satisfy Herbert's $4 million debt to her. House has a swimming pool, an elevator, a wine cellar and a potting shed in the shape of a Japanese tea house. Probably worth $6 million.

HAFT, ROBERT
2346 Massachusetts Ave. NW, DC 20008 (Kalorama Heights)
Tossed out of Dart Group along with mother and sister by father **HERBERT.** Now trying to regain control.

HAFT, RONALD
2435 California St. NW, DC 20008 (Kalorama Heights)
He sided with father **HERBERT** against his mother and siblings, and now he's estranged from all family members.

HECHINGER, JOHN W.
2838 Chain Bridge Rd. NW, DC 20016 (Palisades)
Retired president of Hechinger Co., a northeastern chain of home-building supply stores.

HORNE, LENA
2029 Connecticut Ave. NW, DC 20008 (Kalorama Heights)
Legendary singer.

JOHNSON, ROBERT L.
2915 Audubon Ter., DC 20008 (Forest Hills)
Chairman and founder, Black Entertainment TV—largest African–American–oriented cable television network. Owns 50 percent of stock.

JURGENSEN, SONNY
9321 Old Mansion Road, Mt. Vernon, VA 22121
Former Redskins star and current sports commentator. Real name: Christian Adolph Jurgensen III.

KOGOD, ROBERT
2929 Massachusetts Ave. NW, DC 20008 (Massachusetts Heights)
Heir to Charles E. Smith Company, Washington DC's largest owner of office and residential buildings.

LANGHART, JANET
Market Square Apts., 701 Pennsylvania Ave. NW, DC 20004
   (Downtown)
Black Entertainment Network celebrity, engaged to US Senator (R) from Maine Bill Cohen.

Samuel Lehrman residence

LEHRMAN, SAMUEL M.
2900 Benton Pl. NW, DC 20008 (Massachusetts Heights)
Real estate investor and one of the heirs to Giant Food. Bought house for $4.25 million.

LUSK, RUFUS
Watergate, 2500 Virginia Ave. NW, DC 20037 (Foggy Bottom)
Son of founder of Lusk real estate information company.

MARRIOTT, ALICE (MRS. JOHN WILLARD)
4500 Garfield St. NW, DC 20007 (Wesley Heights)
Co–founder and matriarch of Marriott companies. Also has house in Mirror Lake, NH.

MARRIOTT, BILL (JOHN WILLARD JR.)
7124 Natalli Woods Ln., Potomac, MD 20854
Chairman, president, CEO of Marriott International. Wife Donna had

new tennis court resurfaced because she felt the color was wrong. Like mother, also has house in Mirror Lake, NH

MARRIOTT, RICHARD
10840 Pleasant Hill Dr., Potomac, MD 20854
Chairman, Host Marriott and First Media Co. Also has Mirror Lake, NH and Park City, UT residences.

MARS, FORREST E. JR.
1401 N. Oak St., Arlington, VA 22209
Eldest of three siblings who inherited Mars, Inc., a $12 billion candy/pet food/rice business.

MARS, JACKIE
Watergate East, 2500 Virginia Ave. NW, DC 20037 (Foggy Bottom)
Only daughter of candy king Forrest Sr. (now 91 and living in Miami). Jackie's Watergate apartment is next door to **ROBERT STRAUSS'S** (see POLITICOS). She also has estate, Stonehall Farm, in The Plains, VA outside Middleburg.

MELLON, PAUL
3055 Whitehaven St., DC 20008 (Georgetown)
Philanthropist who has given $671 million in gifts, art collector and gentleman farmer. Also has estate in Upperville, VA worth about $10 million. Father donated National Gallery of Art to Smithsonian.

Paul Mellon residence

MERKERSON, S. EPATHA
5291 W. Boniwood Turnpike, Clinton, MD 20735
This actress plays the no–nonsense NYPD Lt. Anita Van Buren on NBC's "Law & Order." She is married to Toussaint L. Jones, a District of Columbia social worker.

MONK, ART
8251 Greensboro Dr., McLean, Virginia 22102
Former Redskins star and current sports commentator.

MOURNING, ALONZO
8019 Cobble Creek Circle, Potomac, MD 20854
Charlotte Hornets star.

NOTO, LOU
7709 Carlton Pl., McLean, VA 22102
CEO Mobil Corp.

OURISMAN, MANDELL
2817 Woodland Dr., DC 20008 (Massachusetts Heights)
Auto mogul bought this French provincial mansion and is completely renovating it.

PHILLIPS, LAUGHLIN
3044 O St. NW, DC 20007 (Georgetown)
Chairman of Phillips Collection (of art), scion of Phillips steel family.

Laughlin Phillips residence

POLLIN, ABE
2 Goldsboro Ct., Bethesda, MD 20817
Apartment builder and real estate developer who owns Washington Bullets basketball and Washington Capitals hockey teams. Built US Air Arena, formerly called Capital Centre, controls Patriot Center and Baltimore Arena. Also has 226–acre estate in Middleburg, VA.

RUSSELL, MARK
3201 33rd Pl. NW, DC 20008 (Cleveland Park)
Political humorist often seen on public television. His license plate appropriately reads: WASH DC.

SAUL, B. FRANCIS II
One Quincy St., Chevy Chase, MD 20815
Real estate and banking companies, including Chevy Chase Federal Savings Bank. Third generation of B.F. Saul Company, privately owned.

SIMPSON, DONNIE
9608 Conestoga Way, Potomac, MD 20854
DJ on WPGC, VJ on Black Entertainment Television. Instrumental in promoting African–American musicians.

TAGLIABUE, PAUL
5704 Bent Branch Rd., Bethesda, MD 20816
NFL commissioner.

TAUBER, LASZLO
1150 Democracy Blvd., Potomac, MD 20854
Holocaust survivor who came to US with no money, no English. Became a plastic surgeon, invested spectacularly in real estate.

THOMPSON, JOHN R.
4881 Colorado Ave. NW, DC 20011 (Crestwood)
Georgetown Hoyas basketball coach.

TYSON, MIKE
8313 Persimmon Tree Rd., Bethesda, MD 20817
   (Heading west on Persimmon Tree, look for cul-de-sac on right about a half mile before Bradley Blvd.)
Former heavyweight boxing champion and convicted rapist paid $2 million in cash for this mansion on 2.4 acres overlooking Congressional Golf Course. Also has homes in Las Vegas and Cleveland, Ohio, his principal residence until his probationary period ends.

From the Past

★ Please note: Some of the celebrities listed in this chapter no longer live at these addresses. The names of those who still live in or rent these residences, or whose parents still live here, are starred.

AGNEW, SPIRO
2660 Woodley Rd. NW, DC 20008 (Woodley Park)
Where he lived as vice president and where he faced bribery and extortion charges from his time as governor of Maryland. While living in this house, he resigned from vice presidency and pleaded no contest to a tax evasion charge in exchange for assurances that he would not be imprisoned.

AMES, ALDRICH
2512 N. Randolph St., Arlington, VA 22207

CIA mole who was arrested at this house. Now occupied by new owners, who paid $401,000 for it.

Aldrich Ames former residence

ASPIN, LES
2721 O St. NW, DC 20007 (Georgetown)
Late first Secretary of Defense under Clinton who also had been a member of Congress (D–WI) for 22 years.

BAKER, JAMES
2145 Foxhall Rd. NW, DC 20007 (Foxhall)
His residence while US State Dept. secretary under George Bush. Now partner in Baker & Botts law firm.

BEATTY, WARREN/MACLAINE, SHIRLEY
930 N. Liberty St., Arlington, VA 22205
Movie star siblings lived here as kids from 1937 to 50s.

BEREZDEN, RICHARD
3300 Nebraska Ave. NW, DC 200016 (Spring Valley)
College president who made obscene phone calls, not realizing he was calling a police officer's wife.

BERNSTEIN, CARL
1940 Biltmore St. NW, DC (Adams–Morgan)
With **BOB WOODWARD** (see below & MEDIA), broke the Watergate scandal for the *Washington Post*. This was his home then.

BLATTY, WILLIAM PETER
3618 Prospect Pl. NW, DC 20007 (Georgetown)
Exorcist author and screenplay writer. His modern house is located a few houses west of the 39 steep steps leading down to M St., where Father Damien was thrown by the demon. (See also MOVIES, "The Exorcist.")

BOBBITT, JOHN/LORENA
7712 Pine St., Manhassas, VA 22111
Where the couple severed their relationship. Lorena lobbed John's penis out the window at the intersection of Old Centreville Road and Maplewood Drive.

★ BORK, ROBERT
5171 Palisade Ln., Washington, DC 20016 (Palisades)
Failed to win Supreme Court position and, in the process, his name became a verb. According to **WILLIAM SAFIRE** (see MEDIA) in *Safire's New Political Dictionary*, to "bork" is to "attack viciously a candidate or appointee, especially by misrepresentation in the media." Frank Rich of the *New York Times* (who now lives in New York but grew up in northwest Washington) has disagreed, saying the

FROM THE PAST

★ BRENNAN, WILLIAM JOSEPH
1300 Crystal Dr., Arlington, VA 22202
Retired Associate Justice, US Supreme Court.

BRZEZINSKI, ZBIGNIEW
1601 Spring Hill Rd., McLean, VA 22102
Assistant to the President for National Security Affairs under Jimmy Carter.

★ BULLOCK, SANDRA
2925 26th St. N., Arlington VA 22207
Actress who starred in movie "Speed" grew up in this house, where her parents John, a voice coach, and Helga, an opera singer, still live.

BURGER, WARREN
2456 N. Wakefield Ct., Arlington, VA 22207
Late US Supreme Court Associate Justice who resigned to head the US Bicentennial celebration.

Late Warren Burger residence

CASEY, WILLIAM
Tilden Garden Apts., 3020 Tilden St. NW, DC 20008 (Tenley)
Late CIA director during Iran–Contra scandal who allegedly told **BOB WOODWARD** (see MEDIA and below) "I believe" while in hospital's intensive care unit.

★ COLBY, WILLIAM
3028 Dent Pl. NW, DC 20007 (Georgetown)
CIA director during Bush administration. On his watch, we got **ALDRICH AMES** (above).

COOKE, JANET
Ontario Bld. # 122, 1718 P St. NW, DC 20036 (Adams–Morgan)
Former home to the deposed *Washington Post* Pulitzer Prize winner who fabricated the story of Jimmy, an eight-year-old heroin addict. Ironically, she then lived five floors down from **BOB WOODWARD** (see MEDIA and below) of Watergate fame.

★ COURIC, KATIE
4606 40th St. N, Arlington, VA 22207
The house where the "Today Show" host grew up. Her folks still live here.

FORD, JERRY/BETTY
514 Crown View Dr., Alexandria, VA 22314
Where the couple lived from 1955 to 1974, before he replaced **SPIRO AGNEW** (above) as **NIXON'S** (below) vice president.

★ GORE, AL/TIPPER
1201 26th St. S., Arlington, VA 22202
Where they lived before moving to the vice presidential mansion. Had been Tipper's childhood home and is still owned by the Gores; now rented to relatives.

Al/Tipper Gore former residence

★ HAIG, ALEXANDER
6041 Crimson Ct., McLean, VA 22101 (Wesley Heights)
Former US Secretary of State under Ronald Reagan and the man "in control here" after the assassination attempt on Reagan.

HART, GARY
517 6th St. SE, DC 20003 (Capitol Hill)
Where the former US Senator from Colorado, running in the presidential primary, was caught with Donna Rice by *Miami Herald* reporters.

★ HELMS, RICHARD
4649 Garfield St. NW, DC 20007 (Wesley Heights)
Former CIA director under **NIXON,** below.

HOOVER, J. EDGAR
4936 30th Pl. NW, DC 20008 (Forest Hills)
Late FBI director lived here from 1940 until death in 1972. Hoover kept files on Supreme Court justices, members of Congress and US presidents in this house. Current owners had bulletproof–glass windows removed.

JOHNSON, LYNDON/LADY BIRD
The Elms, 4040 52nd St. NW, DC 20016 (Spring Valley)
Where the couple lived while Lyndon was Senator (D) from Texas, then US Vice President.

★ KENNEDY, ETHEL
Hickory Hill, 1147 Chain Bridge Rd., McLean, VA 22101
Widow of RFK still lives on this famous estate.

KENNEDY, JACK/JACKIE
3307 N St. NW, DC 20007 (Georgetown)
Where the couple lived from 1957–1961, while Jack was Senator from Massachusetts, and immediately before moving into White House.

★ KOOP, C. EVERETT
5924 Maplewood Park Place, Bethesda, MD 20814
Bearded former US Surgeon General.

LEONARD, SUGAR RAY
10415 Stapleford Hall Dr., Potomac, MD 20854
Boxing champion lived here during last years of marriage to Juanita. Nine–bedroom turreted castle with stained glass windows; pool with tiles reading "R. & J. Leonard"; professional weight room with motto on wall: "I will win because you don't think I can." Sold house in 1995.

MACLAINE, SHIRLEY see BEATTY, WARREN (above)

MARSHALL, THURGOOD
6233 Lakeview Dr., Falls Church, VA 22041
Late Associate Justice, US Supreme Court; first African American on Court.

★ MCCARTHY, EUGENE
8940 Walker St., Fairfax, VA 22032
Former US Senator (D) from Minnesota and presidential primary candidate; hero of the 60s anti–war movement.

★ MCGOVERN, GEORGE
4012 Linnean Ave. NW, DC 20008 (Forest Hills)
Former US Senator (D) from South Dakota, nominee to presidency in 1972 who lost to **RICHARD NIXON** (below).

★ MCNAMARA, ROBERT
2412 Tracy Pl. NW, DC 20008 (Kalorama Heights)
"Mea culpa" former Secretary of Defense under LBJ, above, helped bring us the Vietnam war. Retired head of World Bank. Also has 41 choice acres on the Martha's Vineyard shoreline.

★ MEESE, ED III
1075 Spring Hill Rd., McLean, VA 22102
Former Attorney General under Ronald Reagan; implicated in WedTech scandal.

MUNDY, KEN
9451 E. Bexhill Dr., Kensington, MD 20895
Late attorney who defended **MARION BARRY** (see POLTICOS) against drug charges.

MURROW, EDWARD R.
5171 Manning Pl. NW, DC 20016 (Foxhall)
Murrow lived here while heading US Information Agency under **JFK** (above). When he learned he had terminal lung cancer, he retired and moved to California. Died on same day that Surgeon General's report was issued linking cigarette smoking to lung cancer.

NIXON, RICHARD/PAT
4308 Forest Ln. NW, DC 20007 (Wesley Heights) and 4801 Tilden St. NW, 20016 DC (Spring Valley)
The first address is where the family lived during the vice presidential years 1957–1960, and the second is where they lived from 1952–1956, also during the vice presidency.

★ PACKWOOD, BOB
Sutton Towers Apts., 3101 New Mexico Ave. NW, DC 20016 (Wesley Heights)
Former US Senator (R) from Washington, tarred by sexual harassment charges. He must enjoy his condo's hot tub.

★ POWELL, LEWIS F. JR.
550 N St. SW, DC 20024 (Waterfront)
Retired Associate Justice, US Supreme Court.

RAY, ELIZABETH
1300 Army–Navy Dr., Arlington, VA 22202
Ray's apartment was frequently visited by her paramour and employer, US Rep. Wayne Hays.

★ SCOWCROFT, BRENT
6114 Wynnwood Rd., Bethesda, MD 20816
National Security adviser under George Bush.

★ SHRIVER, SARGEANT/EUNICE
9109 Harrington Dr., Potomac, MD 20854
He started up the Peace Corps and later was US Ambassador to France; she is **JFK's** sister who founded Special Olympics. Daughter Maria and husband Arnold Schwarzenegger visit frequently.

★ STALLONE, SYLVESTER
10606 Tanager Ln., Potomac, MD 20854
Sly spent part of his early life in Silver Spring, later bought this house for his father and visits frequently.

STEWART, POTTER
5137 Palisade Ln. NW, DC 20016 (Palisades)
Still the residence of the widow of the US Supreme Court justice.

TAYLOR, ELIZABETH
3240 S St. NW, DC 20007 (Georgetown)
Local residence of movie star while married to US Senator from Virginia **JOHN WARNER** (see POLITICOS).

Liz Taylor former residence

THOMAS, CLARENCE
6665 Rutledge Dr., Fairfax, VA 22039
Where he lived during Supreme Court nomination proceedings.

★ TRACHT, DOUG "GREASEMAN"
8 Sandalfoot Ct., Potomac, MD 20854 Outrageous radio DJ with syndicated show. Since 1993, based in Los Angeles. Did you know his middle name is Alfred? Stops here when in town.

★ WEBSTER, WILLIAM
9409 Brooke Dr., Bethesda, MD 20817
Headed CIA during Bush administration.

★ WHITE, BYRON R.
6801 Hampshire Rd., McLean, VA 22101
Retired Associate Justice, US Supreme Court.

★ WOLF, WARNER
11811 Piney Glen Ln., Potomac, MD 20854
Former WUSA TV sportscaster.

WOODWARD, BOB
Ontario Bld. #617, 1718 P St. NW, DC 20036 (Adams–Morgan)
Woodward's apartment during the Watergate investigation. Had the infamous flower pot on the deck moved whenever a message needed to be delivered to Deep Throat. Movie "All The President's Men" placed Woodward in apt. #519, which is incorrect. (See current address, MEDIA.)

★ WOOLSEY, JAMES
6808 Florida St., Chevy Chase, MD 20815
First CIA director under Clinton.

Movie Locations

THE AMERICAN PRESIDENT

Hay–Adams rooftop, One Lafayette Sq. NW, DC (Downtown)
 Establishing shots of exterior WHITE HOUSE AND MALL area were filmed from here.

Greenworks Florist, Willard Hotel, 1455 Pennsylvania Ave. NW, DC (Downtown)
 FLORIST scene.

Cato Institute, 1000 Massachusetts Ave. NW, DC (Dupont Circle)
 The GDC building where environmentalist ANNETTE BENING WORKED. The director added a last–minute evening scene to the movie because the building is so attractive at night.

FORREST GUMP

Independence & 3rd streets SW, DC (Capitol Hill)
 Scene with BLACK PANTHERS showing Capitol in background was shot from the street. Scaffolding was constructed and a piece of scenery was placed on top. The scenery included a false wall with a window; thus, the view.

Calvert St. & Jefferson Davis Highway (Rte. 1), Alexandria, VA
 Exterior of Black Panther's HEADQUARTERS was shot here.

Watergate Hotel, 2650 Virginia Ave. NW, DC (Foggy Bottom)
 Scene at WATERGATE. The entire building was brightly lit for the scene and so filmmakers had to get permission from every other building in the area.

TRUE LIES

Georgetown Park Mall, Wisconsin & M streets NW, DC
 (Georgetown)
 INDOOR SHOPPING CENTER scene. (See **TIMECOP** below.)

K St. NW, around Franklin Park, between 13th &14th streets, DC
 (Franklin Square)
 Outdoor scene with ARNOLD SCHWARZENEGGER ON HORSEBACK. As the scene segues indoors, Schwarzenegger rides his horse through the lobby of Mayflower Hotel, 1127 Connecticut Ave. NW.

Szechuan Gallery Restaurant, 617 H St. NW, DC (Chinatown)
 The Chinese restaurant where JAMIE LEE CURTIS IS SEDUCED.

New York Avenue NW & 3rd St. NW, DC (Ledroit)
 USED CAR LOT scenes.

The MARRIOTT MARQUIS scene was actually located at that hotel in Manhattan.

IN THE LINE OF FIRE

California St. NW between 18th & 19th streets NW, DC
 (Adams–Morgan)
 Scene where CLINT EASTWOOD CHASES JOHN MALKOVITCH, Eastwood jumps from 1860 California St. over alley to 1858, and hangs from roof of 1858 California St.

East Capitol & 2nd streets NE, DC (Capitol Hill)
 Another CHASE scene.

A FEW GOOD MEN

St. Elizabeths Hospital, DC (Congress Heights)
    NAVY ADMINISTRATION scenes shot on hospital campus.

20th St. NW & Belmont Pl. NW, DC (Adams–Morgan)
    The outdoor scene with BABY CARRIAGE.

TIMECOP

Georgetown Park Mall, Wisconsin & M streets NW, DC
        (Georgetown)
    First scene in movie WITH JEAN–CLAUDE VAN DAMME. (See **TRUE LIES**, above.)

DAVE

1737 Kenyon St. NW, DC (Mount Pleasant)
    Where KEVIN KLINE lived.

Post Office Building, 12th & Constitution streets NW, DC
        (Downtown)
    The exterior scene where Dave is rushed out of the Capitol after feigning a HEART ATTACK was filmed here. The entrance was made to look like the steps of the Capitol building.

2431 18th St. NW, DC (Adams–Morgan)
    Dave and First Lady (Signourey Weaver) are STOPPED BY COPS. You can see Cafe Lautrec and Argentine Grill in the shot.

1442 Wisconsin Ave. NW, DC (Georgetown)
    Location of Dave's EMPLOYMENT AGENCY. Now a clothing store.

CLEAR AND PRESENT DANGER

Northumberland, 2039 New Hampshire Ave. NW, DC (Dupont Circle)
DEMI MOORE'S apartment. (See **BROADCAST NEWS,** below.)

2039 Massachusetts Ave. NW, DC (Kalorama Heights)
The SECRETARY'S apartment house.

PELICAN BRIEF

Riggs Bank, 1503 Pennsylvania Ave. NW, DC (Downtown)
SAFETY DEPOSIT scene in bank.

Warner Theatre Lobby, 1299 Pennsylvania Ave. NW, DC (Downtown)
LOBBY scene.

Ben's Chili Bowl, 1213 U St. NW, DC (Shaw)
DENZEL WASHINGTON MET WITH WHITE HOUSE GUARD at Ben's.

Public Garage, Old Georgetown Rd, bounded by Woodmont Ave. & Edgemoor Ln., Bethesda, MD
PARKING GARAGE scene.

THE FIRM

US Department of Commerce, 15th & Constitution streets NW, DC (Downtown)
The OFFICE OF THE FBI CHIEF was shot here because of its great window view of the Washington Monument.

SILENCE OF THE LAMBS

Office of the Secretary, US Department of Labor, Room 203, 200 Constitution Ave., DC (Downtown)
FBI DIRECTOR'S OFFICE was shot in the office of the Secretary. Nearly all movies with Washington scenes that show the Capitol Building through the window of a government office are shot in this room.

NO WAY OUT

Whitehurst Freeway, NW, DC (Georgetown)
CAR CHASE took place along the Freeway.

C&O Canal, DC (Georgetown)
KEVIN COSTNER JOGGED along C&O Canal.

GEORGETOWN SUBWAY location was actually shot in the Baltimore subway.

BROADCAST NEWS

Northumberland, Apt. 301, 2039 New Hampshire Ave. NW, DC (Dupont Circle)
WILLIAM HURT'S apartment. (See **CLEAR AND PRESENT DANGER,** above.)

600 East Capitol St. SE, DC (Capitol Hill)
ALBERT BROOKS' house.

Hillyer Pl., NW, DC (Dupont Circle)
Street where HOLLY HUNTER LIVED. This street was chosen for exterior scenes because it is only one block long and traffic could easily be controlled.

EXORCIST 3

Ascension & St. Agnes Church, Massachusetts Ave. & 12th St. NW, DC (Downtown)
   Infamous CHURCH THAT EXPLODED in movie is still standing at corner.

EXORCIST

Prospect St. and 36th St. NW, DC (Georgetown)
   The demon took up residence in a very swank section of Georgetown. The actual movie house was a stage set. (For author Blatty's address on this street, see PAST.) Note the STEEP STEPS NEARBY, WHERE FATHER DAMIEN WAS THROWN TO HIS DEATH. Ironically, these steps—39 in all—used to be nicknamed the Hitchcock steps, in reference to his movie "The 39 Steps." Other outdoor scenes were shot on the nearby Georgetown University campus.

The Playing Fields

EATING SPOTS AND NIGHTCLUBS

ANDALUSIAN DOG
1344 U St. NW, DC (Adams–Morgan)
202–986–6364
Catch Andrew Sullivan, editor of *The New Republic,* here.

AUSTIN GRILL
2404 Wisconsin Ave. NW, DC (Tenley)
202–337–8080
The **HAFT** family members eat here, although not as a group anymore.

BLUES ALLEY
1073 Wisconsin Ave. NW, DC (Georgetown)
202–337–4141
Washington's preeminent jazz spot. Any time bluesmen or women are in town, they spend an evening here.

BOMBAY CLUB RESTAURANT
815 Connecticut Avenue NW, DC (Downtown)
202–659–3727
On several evenings, the Clinton family has strolled across Lafayette Square to dine here. Also a favorite both with White House aides and the *New York Times* news bureau.

BULLFEATHERS OF CAPITOL HILL
410 First St. SE, DC (Capitol Hill)
202–543–5005
Where you can find the GOP faithful.

CAFE ATLANTICO
1819 Columbia Road NW, DC (Adams–Morgan)
202–328–5844
Great food, and then when dinner is over, the tables are pushed to one side to make room for the suave Latin crowd strutting their stuff.

CAFE LAUTREC
2431 18th St. NW, DC (Adams–Morgan)
202–265–6436
You can spot many young Clinton appointees in this cafe because they live in nearby Adams–Morgan or Dupont Circle.

CAFE MILANO
3251 Prospect St., DC (Georgetown)
202–333–6183
If you like foreign accents, check out Milano's EuroFlash. This restaurant is where Marlene Ramallo, the sort–of wife of billionaire Redskins owner **JACK KENT COOKE,** was drinking before she drove through Georgetown with a man sprawled on the hood of her Jaguar.

CAPITAL BAR AT THE CAPITAL HOTEL
1001 16th St. NW, DC (Downtown)
202–393–1000
JOHNNY APPLE, Washington–bureau chief of the *New York Times,* drinks here with other print media types and network bigwigs. The heaviest drinkers are the reporters from the British tabloids.

THE CAPITAL GRILLE
601 Pennsylvania Ave. NW, DC (Downtown)
202-737-6200
Jammed with members of Congress, lobbyists and attorneys, especially if they're Republicans. AG **JANET RENO** also likes this place.

CHICKEN–OUT ROTISSERIE
10116–B River Road, Potomac, MD
301–299–8585
RICHARD MARRIOTT rollerblades to this casual eatery, removes his skates and sits down to eat in stocking feet.

CITY LIGHTS OF CHINA
1731 Connecticut Ave. NW, DC (Dupont Circle)
202–265–6688
Model Jerry Hall and Rolling Stones pals Mick Jagger and Charlie Watts eat at this Chinese restaurant when in town.

CLYDE'S OF GEORGETOWN
3236 M St., DC (Georgetown)
202–333–9180
This restaurant popularized Georgetown as an eating spot. In the 70s, its happy hour menu was called "Afternoon Delights," and the phrase served as the basis of Starland Vocal Band's hit song by that name. Starlight's gold record hangs on Clyde's wall.

COCO LOCO
810 7th St. NW, DC (Downtown)
202–289–2626
Currently has the edge over Cafe Atlantico for the international "beautiful people" who come here for Latin dancing and expensive drinks.

FETTOOSH RESTAURANT
3277 M St. NW, DC (Georgetown)
202–342–1199
Look for HHS Secretary **DONNA SHALALA,** of Lebanese heritage, chowing down on this Lebanese cuisine with friend Attorney General **JANET RENO.**

FLEETWOOD'S RESTAURANT AND BLUES CLUB
44 Canal Center Plaza, Alexandria, VA
703–548–6425
A new jazz club owned by Mick Fleetwood, founder of Fleetwood Mac. Bonnie Raitt stops by when she's in town. You can also catch a bipartisan crowd here: GOP National Committee chair Haley Barbour and Virginia State Democratic chair Mark Warner come in frequently—they're both investors in the club.

FLORIDA AVENUE GRILL
1100 Florida Ave. NW, DC (Cardoza)
202–265–1586
Near Howard University, this everyman restaurant hosts Associate Justice **CLARENCE THOMAS,** US Supreme Court.

GALILEO RESTAURANT
1110 21st St. NW, DC (Downtown)
202–293–7191
When US Ambassador to France **PAMELA HARRIMAN** is in town and craves Italian, she dines here.

GEORGIA BROWN'S
950 15th St. NW, DC (Downtown)
202-393-4499
Nice mix of such black and white powerbrokers as **JESSE JACKSON** and **SAM NUNN**. Table 80, at the center, is the premiere spot. Table 81 is **VERNON JORDAN'S**.

GERMAINE'S ASIAN CUISINE
2400 Wisconsin Ave. NW, DC (Upper Georgetown)
202-965-1185
You can catch Secretary of State Warren Christopher and Energy Secretary **HAZEL O'LEARY** here, along with **VERNON JORDAN** and **TIPPER GORE**. Stars **WARREN BEATTY** and Jack Nicholson also like Germaine's Vietnamese/Southeast Asian cuisine.

HAWK & DOVE RESTAURANT
329 Pennsylvania Ave. SE, DC (Capitol Hill)
202-543-3300
Where you might catch your congressperson having a drink while waiting for the roll call.

HERB'S RESTAURANT
1615 Rhode Island Ave. NW, DC (Adams-Morgan)
202-333-4372
Don't let its Holiday Inn facade fool you—this is where the literary lions and the actors from Arena Stage gather.

THE IMPROV
1140 Connecticut Ave. NW, DC (Downtown)
202-296-7008
Comedy club. Vice President **AL GORE** shows up when Bob Somerby, a political comedian, is headlined: Al, Somerby and actor Tommy Lee Jones were Harvard roommates 25 years ago.

JALEO
480 7th St. NW, DC (Downtown)
202-628-7949
A tapas bar frequented by Rep. Rosa DeLauro and husband Stan Greenberg, the Democratic pollster.

JOCKEY CLUB RESTAURANT
Ritz Carlton Hotel, 2100 Massachusetts Ave. NW, DC (Kalorama Heights)
202–659–8000
Still the In spot for Ladies Who Lunch, although its popularity has waned since its crest during the Reagan administration.

KINKEAD'S RESTAURANT
2000 Pennsylvania Ave. DC (Downtown)
202–286–7700
Catch **ANTHONY LAKE,** National Security Advisor and his colleague Warren Christopher, US Secretary of State, here.

LA BRASSERIE
239 Massachusetts Ave. NE, DC (Capitol Hill)
202–546–9154
Where **TED KENNEDY** allegedly had sex with a blonde on a table top. Chances are slim that he returns to dine here with his new wife, Vickie. But JFK Jr. still comes in. You can also spot Bob Tyrrell, king of conservatism and editor of *American Spectator*. Once a month, he brings in such journalists as **P.J. O'ROURKE** and Bob Novak for political discussions.

LA COLLINE
400 N. Capitol St. NW, DC (Capitol Hill)
202–737–0400
The lobbyists lunch here. Conveniently situated under National Association of Governors.

MILLIE & AL'S
2440 18th St. NW, DC (Adams–Morgan)
202–387–8131
A favorite with the younger Clinton Crowd.

MONOCLE ON CAPITOL HILL
107 D St. NE, DC (Capitol Hill)
202–546–4488
Senators and Supreme Court justices prefer this restaurant for lunch.

MORTON'S OF CHICAGO–THE STEAKHOUSE
3251 Prospect St. NW, DC (Georgetown)
202–342–6258
Washington has both the Palm and this great steakhouse. Dan Rostenkowski is honored with a brass plaque reading "Rosty's Rotunda" that marks his favorite table. Good thing Rosty doesn't let his 17 indictments on fraud and embezzlement spoil his appetite.

MR. K'S RESTAURANT
2121 K. St. NW, DC (Downtown)
202–331–8868
The **DOLES** eat here almost every night.

MY BROTHER'S PLACE
130 C St. NW, DC (Downtown)
202–347–1350
Where the young GOP faithful drink and eat.

NORA RESTAURANT
2132 Florida Ave. NW, DC (Dupont Circle)
202–462–5143
Bill and Hillary eat here. Nora's is also a favorite of the media.

OLD EBBITT GRILL
675 15th St. NW, DC (Downtown)
202–347–4800
Leon Panetta walks a few blocks from his White House office to eat at this historic restaurant. Clyde's chili is served but Barbra Streisand and Aretha Franklin prefer to send for its take–out.

THE ORIGINAL PANCAKE HOUSE
7700 Wisconsin Ave., Bethesda, MD
301–986–0285
Bethesda and northwest DC are the sites of many broadcasting towers because the land is the highest in the metropolitan area. The TV and radio gang, including Helen Thomas of nearby UPI, head here for breakfast and lunch.

PALM RESTAURANT
1225 19th St. NW, DC (Dupont Circle)
202-293-9091
A haunt of the rich and powerful who have appetites big enough for the huge chops and steaks. Regulars are Rep. Dan Rostenkowski, **LARRY KING,** Mary Matalin and James Carville, and radio personality Don Imus. Also, new Redskins coach Norv Turner and former coach Joe Gibbs use The Palm as their training table. Tipper Gore occasionally gives staff parties here.

PIZZERIA PARADISO
2029 P St. NW, DC (Dupont Circle)
202-223-1245
Has young, hip—for Washington—patrons. Also popular with the younger members of Clinton's Crowd.

RED RIVER GRILL
201 Massachusetts Ave. NE, DC (Capitol Hill)
202-546-7200
Spot members of Congress and their staff having lunch or afternoon drinks. Senator Carol Moseley-Braun of Illinois is a regular.

SAIGON INN
2928 M St. NW, DC (Georgetown)
202-337-5588
While others dine on wonderful food, Jane Fonda sticks to black coffee.

SEQUOIA RESTAURANT
3000 K St. NW, DC (Georgetown) (The portion of K Street under the Whitehurst Expressway, also known as Water Street NW)
202-944-4200
Where the Clintons occasionally have Sunday brunch. On a warm evening, try the outdoor bar overlooking the Potomac River and see Washington at its most lovely.

SESTO SENSO ITALIAN RESTAURANT
1214 18th St., DC (Dupont Circle)
202-785-9525
If you're as rich as Mick Jagger, you, too, can tip your Italian waiter $100.

TRACKS DC
80 M St. SE, DC (Navy Yard)
202–488–3320
Who's gay in Congressional offices or in the Clinton administration? Check it out here.

VENEZIANO
2305 18th St. NW DC (Adams–Morgan)
202–483–9300
This trendy Italian restaurant has played host to President Clinton, who will hop from table to table greeting other diners.

WAGSHAL'S DELICATESSEN
4855 Massachusetts Ave., DC (Spring Valley)
202–363–5698
Although the original owners have retired, Wagshal's continues to be Washington's best delicatessen. Just ask George and Barbara Bush, who used to send Secret Service agents to pick up sandwiches for them.

HOTELS

FOUR SEASONS HOTEL
2828 Pennsylvania Ave. NW, DC (Downtown)
202-342-0444
Posh hotel where Sharon Stone stays when she visits. Concierge has a wealth of information on this city.

HAY-ADAMS HOTEL
One Lafayette Square, DC (Downtown)
202-638-6600
Historic hotel lodges many out-of-town White House dinner guests, and even past and future White House residents—Hillary and Bill Clinton stayed here during the transition period at the end of 1992. Several years earlier, Ollie North used its bar and resturant as staging areas for Contra fundraising.

HOWARD JOHNSON MOTOR LODGE
2601 Virginia Ave. NW, DC (Foggy Bottom)
202-965-2700
Always popular due to its history. From room 419, the Plumbers, hired by the Attorney General John Mitchell of the Committee to Re-elect the President, monitored phone calls of the Democratic National Committee, which was across the street in the Watergate Hotel. Before the DNC break-in, the Plumbers moved to room 723 to see better. Even though they radioed their partners inside the DNC that a guard was coming, the burglars were caught and arrested.

STOUFFER MAYFLOWER HOTEL
1127 Connecticut Ave. NW, DC (Downtown)
202-327-3000
The lobby is a popular place for short business meetings. JFK, when living at the White House, retained suite 812 for his assignations.

PARK HYATT HOTEL
1201 24th St. NW, DC (West End)
202-789-1234
This is a lovely new hotel that rock stars prefer: a few years ago, both Robert Plant, formerly of Led Zeppelin, and New Kids on the Block were in suites on the top floor at the same time.

WASHINGTON VISTA HOTEL
1400 M St. NW, DC (Downtown)
202-839-5555
Best known for the popular videotape of Marion Barry's 1990 arrest for crack cocaine possession in room 727.

WILLARD INTERCONTINENTAL HOTEL
1401 Pennsylvania Ave. NW, DC (Downtown)
202-628-9100
Everyone has stayed at the hotel where the term "lobbyist" was coined: Ulysses S. Grant would walk from the White House to the nearby Willard for his cigar and brandy but was irritated by special interest group members who congregated in its lobby, hoping to catch his ear. He complained about the "lobbyists" and the phrase caught on.

WHERE THEY WORK OUT

ST. ALBAN'S TENNIS CLUB
Mount Saint Alban, Wisconsin and Massachusetts Avenues, DC (Cathedral Heights)
202-363-2131
Exclusive club for the Washington Establishment. See WASPites Strobe Talbott (State) and James Woolsey (CIA) play on Sunday mornings.

TONUS STUDIO OF POTOMAC
11325 Seven Locks Rd., Potomac, MD
301-299-5700
Shapely Potomac women can be found here, exercising or stretching in Washington's only Callanetics classes.

WASHINGTON SPORTS CLUB
1835 Connecticut Ave. NW, DC (Dupont Circle)
202-332-0100
Watch George Stephanopoulos, the President's young senior adviser, climb the Stairmaster.

WASHINGTON SPORTS CLUB
214 D St. SE, DC (Capitol Hill)
202-547-2255
Populated by Hill staffers and squash players.

WASHINGTON SPORTS CLUB
2251 Wisconsin Ave. NW, DC (Glover Park)
202-333-2323
The chefs and owners of the many restaurants in the area, including Austin Grill and Le Caprice, come here to work out.

WEST END FITNESS CENTER
2401 M St. NW, DC (West End)
202-457-5070
Arnold Schwarzenegger and Maria Shriver's gym when they're in town visiting the senior Shrivers' Potomac house.

YMCA
1711 Rhode Island Ave. NW, DC (Adams-Morgan)
202-862-9622
A gorgeous facility with equally good-looking exec types.

BEST PLACE IN WASHINGTON ON AN AUTUMN SUNDAY

OWNER'S BOX, RFK STADIUM
Lincoln Park, DC
Everyone wants to join Jack Kent Cooke in his personal box and watch the Redskins play. When guests get hungry, they can cross the catwalk to the Lombardi Room, also at the disposal of the Redskins owner. Last season, one afternoon's guests included Bob and Ellen Bennett, George McGovern and Johnny Apple.

WHERE THE BEAUTIFUL PEOPLE GET BEAUTIFIED

CHRISTOPHE SALON
1125 18th St. NW, DC (Downtown)
202–785–2222
You can catch the First Family's former hairdresser here when he's not layering planes into holding patterns at LAX. Not for the idle curious, though. Christophe charges $250 per head, although the coffee is complimentary.

CORNROWS & COMPANY
5401 14th St. NW, DC (Downtown)
202–723–1827
California decor and the most successful female buppies can be found here.

THE FOURTH LOCK
3067 Canal Towpath (on the C&O Canal between Thomas Jefferson Pl. and 31st St. NW) DC (Georgetown)
202–342–5625
A favorite with Francophones—everyone from the French Embassy comes here for a tres chic coiffure.

GEORGETTE KLINGER SKIN CARE SALON
5345 Wisconsin Ave. NW, DC (Chevy Chase)
202–686–8880
Hillary Clinton has had her pores minimized by Klinger facialists—who are the best in the business, having proven themselves in Manhattan, Beverly Hills, Palm Beach and other swank locations before coming to Chevy Chase.

ILO DAY SPA
1637 Wisconsin Ave. NW, DC (Georgetown)
202–342–0350
Ethel and Vickie Kennedy go to Ilo. Nephew–in–law Arnold Schwarzenegger comes in for manicures when he's in town. (Shaping and buffing only, of course.)

LUCIEN ET EIVIND COIFFURE
2233 Wisconsin Ave. NW, DC (Upper Georgetown)
202–965–2100
Eivind coifs the blonde locks of Sharon Percy Rockefeller, the golden–honey tresses of Pamela Harriman and the raven mane of Lynda Johnson Robb. Only Lucien knows for sure about Paula Parkinson . . . her hair shade, that is.

NORBERT 1050 Connecticut Ave. NW, DC (Downtown)
202–466–2111
Tipper Gore comes here for a haircut.

OKYO
2903 M St. NW, DC (Georgetown)
202–342–2675
More foreign languages can be heard above the din of the hair blowers than at the United Nations. One of the co–owners, when he lived in France, was Catherine Deneuve's hair colorist.

ROBERT LEWIS SALON
1753 Rockville Pike, Rockville, MD
301–468–0777
Local television sportscaster Jess Atkins has his hair cut here.

ROCHE HAIR, SKIN AND NAILS
2445 M St., DC (West End)
202–775– 0775
Progressive hair stylists to the hip. George Stephanopoulos also has his hair cut here, although not often enough.

SHELTON'S HAIR GALLERY
1215 Connecticut Ave. NW, DC (Downtown)
202–223–8311
This salon styles the hair of both the mayor and his wife.

SYLVAIN MELLOUL SALONS (formerly VISAGE)
Six area locations with home base at 3034 M St. NW, DC
  (Georgetown)
202–965–4421
Since the Clintons dropped Cristophe because of his high–octane image, Sylvan is cutting the First Lady's hair for only $18. For the Hair Cuttery crowd.

DOWNTOWN CLUBS

CITY CLUB
555 13th St. NW, DC (Downtown)
202–347–0818
Members include lawyer/lobbyist Mike Barnes, former congressman from Montgomery County, James Baker, former Secretary of State under Ronald Reagan, Cathleen P. Black, former editor of *USA Today*, Secretary of Commerce Ron Brown, former Brent Scowcroft, lobbyist Anne Wexler.

COSMOS CLUB
2121 Massachusetts Ave. NW, DC (Dupont Circle)
202–387–7783
More than two dozen Nobel laureates or Pulitzer prize winners are members of this club.

F STREET CLUB
1925 F St. NW, DC (Downtown)
202–331–1925
Don't go to the trouble of knocking, they won't let you in.

METROPOLITAN CLUB
1700 H St. NW, DC (Downtown)
202–835–2500
A clout club. CNN reporter Brit Hume is a member.

UNIVERSITY CLUB
1135 16th St. NW, DC (Downtown)
202–862–8800
Wealthy Clinton Crowd member Bob Rubin belongs.

COUNTRY CLUBS

ARMY NAVY COUNTRY CLUB
2400 South 18th St., Arlington, VA
703-521-6800
Not all that prestigious but you might see one of the Joint Chiefs playing golf.

BURNING TREE CLUB
River and Burdette roads, Bethesda, MD
301-365-1200
Where the presidents play. The club gave up its tax-exempt status and raised membership fees rather than admit women as members.

CHEVY CHASE CLUB
6100 Connecticut Ave. NW, Chevy Chase, MD
301-652-4100
A mixture of old money (Mrs. Armistead Peter III) and new (Mandell Ourisman), Republicans (William Bennett, James Baker, William Bradford Reynolds) and Democrats (Clark Clifford and Alan Greenspan). A member of America's wealthiest family, Virginia Mars, holds membership along with the widow of a Supreme Court justice, Mrs. Potter Stewart.

CONGRESSIONAL COUNTRY CLUB
8500 River Rd., Bethesda, MD
301-469-2000
No longer a long waiting list, somewhat family friendly.

KENWOOD GOLF & COUNTRY CLUB
5601 River Rd., Bethesda, MD
301-320-3000
Neighborhood club, albeit a swank neighborhood.

LANGSTON GOLF COURSE
26th St. and Benning Rd. NE, DC (Kingman Park)
202-397-8638
This is the oldest African-American-affiliated golf course in the city. Open to the public.

WOODMONT COUNTRY CLUB
1201 Rockville Pike, Rockville, MD
301-424-7200
This club, known as the "Jewish" country club, has such members as television celebrity Maury Povich and restaurateur Duke Zeibert.

SCHOOLS

HOLTON-ARMS SCHOOL
7303 River Rd., Potomac, MD
301-365-5300
Diplomats and the upwardly mobile send their daughters to Holton. Despite Jackie Onassis' attendance in ninth and tenth grades before she went to Farmington, this school is not as uppercrust as National Cathedral School.

NATIONAL CATHEDRAL SCHOOL FOR GIRLS and ST. ALBANS SCHOOL FOR BOYS
3609 Woodley Rd. NW, DC
202-537-6300 and Wisconsin
and Massachusetts avenues NW, DC
202-537-6435
(Cathedral Heights)
Respectively, the girls' and boys' school of the top-ranked families. The Gore children attend these schools, as did their parents before them. Senator Jay and Sharon Rockefeller's son is also enrolled.

SIDWELL FRIENDS SCHOOL
3825 Wisconsin Ave. NW, DC (Tenley)
202-537-8100
This school, always popular with left-leaners, has risen even higher in standing since Chelsea Clinton jumped over a long waiting list to be enrolled. Media criticism of a liberal president's sending his child to an exclusive private school was muted. Maybe the hushed voices were due to the not-so-coincidental attendance of the children of Howard Fineman *(Newsweek)*, Don Graham and Bob Woodward *(Washington Post)*, and grandchildren of Arthur Ochs Sulzberger *(New York Times)*.

IN WASHINGTON, NO ONE CALLS 911

HUNTEMANN AMBULANCE SERVICE
202–726–5700
Unlike the DC Public Ambulances, Huntemann's will take you to the hospital or physician of your choice. In case they can't help you, go to:

JOSEPH GAWLER'S & SONS
5130 Wisconsin Ave. NW, DC (Chevy Chase)
202–966–6400
The funeral directors who since 1850 have prepared for burial Washington's most famous bodies: Woodrow Wilson, FDR, Dwight Eisenhower, JFK, J. Edgar Hoover, Thurgood Marshall, W. Edwards Deming and Jacqueline Bouvier Onassis have been laid out here.

NAME INDEX

(Where there is more than one reference, bold face = residence)

Agnew, Spiro, **39**, 42
Akaka, Daniel, 15
Albright, Madeline, 11
Alexander, Jane, 11, *ill. 11*
Allbritton, Joseph, 31
Altman, Robert, 15
Ames, Aldrich, 17, **39,** 42, *ill. 39*
Anderson, Jack, 1
Apple, R.W. "Johnny", 1, 56
Aristide, Jean-Bertrand, 13, **15**
Aspin, Les, 39
Babbit, Bruce, 11
Bainum, Stewart Jr., 31
Baker, Howard, 15
Baker, James, 40
Baker, Russell, 1
Baldrige, Letitia, 1
Barry, Marion, **15,** 45
Beatty, Warren, 40, 58
Bennett, Bill, 15
Bennett, Bob, 15
Bentsen, Lloyd, 16
Berezden, Richard, 40
Bernstein, Carl, 40
Billington, James, 11
Bingaman, Jeff, 16
Bingham, Joan, 31
Blatty, William Peter, 40, *ill. 54*
Blitzer, Wolf, 1
Bobbitt, John/Lorena, 40
Boggs, Lindy, 7, **16**
Boggs, Thomas, 7, **16**
Bond, Christopher, 16
Bono, Sonny, 16
Boren, David, 16
Bork, Robert, 40
Bradlee, Ben, 1
Bradley, Bill, 16
Breaux, John, 16
Brennan, William Joseph, 41
Brimmer, Andrew F., 17
Brinkley, David, 2
Brock, David, **2,** 40

73

Broder, David, 2
Brown, J. Carter, 31
Brown, Ron, 12
Bruce, Evangeline, 31
Brzezinski, Zbigniew, 41
Buchanan, Patrick, 2, *ill. 2*
Buchwald, Art, 2
Buckley, Chris, 2
Bullock, Sandra, 41
Bumpers, Dale, 17
Burger, Warren, 41, *ill. 41*
Cacheris, Plato, 17
Cafritz, Calvin, 32
Cafritz, Carter, 32
Cafritz, Conrad/Peggy, 32
Campbell, Ben Nighthorse, 17
Carlucci, Frank, 17
Carr, Oliver T., 32
Carr, Robert O, 32
Carter, Linda: see Altman, Robert
Casey, William, 41
Casserly, Charley, 32
Chafee, John, 17
Cheney, Lynne/Richard, 17
Cisneros, Henry, 12
Clifford, Clark, 17
Clinger, William F. Jr., 18
Cochran, Thad, 18
Colby, William, 42
Cooke, Jack Kent, 17, **32,** 56
Cooke, Janet, 42
Couric, Katie, 42
Coverdell, Paul, **18,** 28
Coyne, Marshall, 33
Cuomo, Andrew/Kerry Kennedy, 12
Cutler, Lloyd, 18
Danforth, John, 18
Davis, Evelyn Y., 33
De Borchgrave, Arnaud, 2
Deconcini, Dennis, 19
Dell, Donald, 33
Dellums, Ronald, 18
Dikembe, Mutombo, 33
Dole, Elizabeth/Robert, 18, 60
Domenici, Pete, 18
Donaldson, Sam, 2
Dorgan, Byron, 19
Downey, Edward M., 3

Downie, Leonard, 3
Duffey, Joseph, 12
Edelman, Marian Wright, 19
Edwards, Don, 19
Evans, Rowland, 3
Ewing, Patrick, 33
Exon, J. James, 19
Feinstein, Dianne, 19
Feld, Kenneth, 33
Foley, Mark, 19
Foley, Tom, 19
Ford, Betty/Jerry, 42
Ford, Wendell, 19
Friedan, Betty, 3
Frist, Bill, 19
Gephardt, Richard, 20
Gergen, David, 20
Gingrich, Newt, **20,** 21, *ill. 20*
Ginsburg, Ruth Bader, 20
Glickman, Dan, 12
Gonzalez, Henry, 20
Gore, Al Jr./Tipper, 20, **42,** 58. 61, *ill. 42*
Gore, Al Sr., **21,** 20, *ill. 20*
Gorton, Slade, 21
Graham, Donald E., 3
Graham, Katharine, 1, **3**
Gramm, Phil/Wendy, 21
"Greaseman": *see* Tracht, Doug
Green, Darrell, 33
Greenspan, Alan, 21
Grosvenor, Gilbert M., 3
Haft, Gloria, **33,** 34, 55
Haft, Herbert, 33, **34,** 55
Haft, Linda, 33
Haft, Robert, 34
Haft, Ronald, 34
Haig, Alexander, 43
Harriman, Pamela, 12, 57
Hart, Gary, 43
Haskell, Floyd: *see* Totenberg, Nina
Hatch, Orrin, 21
Hechinger, John W., 34
Heflin, Howell, 21, *ill. 20*
Helms, Jesse, 21
Helms, Richard, 43
Hersh, Seymour, 3
Hitchens, Christopher, 4
Hollings, Ernest, 21

Hoover, J. Edgar, 43
Horne, Lena, 34
Houghton, Amory Jr., 21
Hoyer, Steny, 21
Huffington, Arianna S./Michael, 4
Hughes, Cathy, 4
Hume, Brit, 4
Inouye, Daniel, 22
Jackson, Jesse, 22, 58
Jarvis, Charlene Drew, 22
Jeffords, James, 22
Johnson, Lady Bird/Lyndon, 27, **43**
Johnson, Robert L., 34
Johnston, J. Bennett Jr., 22
Jordan, Vernon E. Jr., 22, 58
Jurgensen, Sonny, 34
Kamber, Vic, 22
Kantor, Mickey, 22
Kassebaum, Nancy, 22
Kelley, Kitty, 4
Kelly, Sharon Pratt, 22
Kemp, Jack, 23
Kendall, David, 12
Kennedy, Anthony, 23, *ill. 23*
Kennedy, Ethel, 6, 12, 23, **43**
Kennedy, Jack/Jackie, 1, 23, **43,** 45, 46
Kennedy, Joseph P. Jr., 13, 15, **23**
Kennedy, Ted, 23, 58
Kessler, Pamela/Ron, 4
King, Larry, 4, 61
Kinsley, Michael, 5, *ill. 5*
Kiplinger, Austin, 5
Kogod, Robert, 35
Koop, C. Everett, 44
Koppel, Ted, 5
Kraft, Polly: *see* Cutler, Lloyd
Kristol, Irving, **5,** 23
Kristol, William, 5, **23**
Lake, Anthony, 13, 59, *ill. 13*
Lamb, Brian P., 24
Langhart, Janet, 35
LaPierre, Wayne R., 24
Leach, Jim, 24
Lehrer, Jim, 5
Lehrman, Samuel M., 35, *ill. 35*
Leonard, Sugar Ray, 44
Levin, Carl, 24, *ill. 24*
Lewis, Delano, 5

Limpert, Jack, 6
Lott, Trent, 24
Lugar, Richard, 24
Lusk, Rufus, 35
MacLaine, Shirley: see Beatty, Warren
Mankiewicz, Frank, 6
Marriott, Alice, 35
Marriott, Bill, 35-36
Marriott, Richard, 36, 56
Mars, Forrest E. Jr., 36
Mars, Jackie, 36
Marshall, Thurgood, 44
Matthews, Chris/Kathleen, 6
McCain, John, 24
McCarthy, Eugene, 44
McClendon, Sarah, 6
McGovern, George, 44
McNamara, Robert, 44
Meese, Ed III, 44
Mellon, Paul, 36, *ill. 36*
Merkerson, S. Epatha, 37
Merrill, Philip, 6
Metzenbaum, Howard, 24
Meyers, Jan, 24
Michel, Robert H., 25
Mitchell, Andrea, 6
Monk, Art, 37
Morella, Connie/Tony, 25
Mourning, Alonzo, 37
Moynihan, Patrick, 25
Mundy, Ken, 45
Murrow, Edward R., 45
Nickles, Don, 25
Nixon, Pat/Richard, 13, 42, 43, 44, **45**
Norton, Eleanor Holmes, 25, *ill. 25*
Noto, Lou, 37
Nunn, Sam, 25, 58
Oberstar, James, 26
Obey, David, 26
O'Leary, Hazel, 13, 58
O'Rourke, P.J., 6, 58
Orth, Maureen, 6
Ourisman, Mandell, 37
Packwood, Bob, 45
Pell, Claiborne, 26
Pena, Federico, 13
Percy, Charles, **26,** 27
Perry, William J., 13

Peterson, Gordon, 7
Phillips, Laughlin, 37, *ill. 37*
Pollin, Abe, 37
Povich, Shirley, 7
Powell, Colin, 26
Powell, Lewis F. Jr., 45
Pressler, Larry, 26
Pryor, David, 26
Quinn, Sally: *see* Bradlee, Ben
Rangel, Charles, 26
Raskin, Barbara, 7
Ray, Elizabeth, 45
Ray, John, 26
Regardie, Bill, 7
Rehnquist, William, 26
Reid, Harry, 27
Reno, Janet, **13,** 15, 56, 57, *ill. 11*
Riley, Richard, 13
Rivlin, Alice, 13
Robb, Chuck/Lynda, 27
Roberts, Cokie/Steve, **7,** 16
Roberts, Pat, 27
Rockefeller, Jay (John D. IV)/Sharon Percy, 27
Rowan, Carl, 7
Rubin, Bob, 14, *ill. 14*
Russell, Mark, 38
Russert, Tim: *see* Orth, Maureen
Safire, William, **7,** 40
Salinger, Pierre, 8
Sasser, James, 27
Saul, B. Francis II, 38
Scalia, Antonin, 23, **27**
Schieffer, Bob, 8
Schorr, Daniel, 8
Schroeder, Patricia, 27
Scowcroft, Brent, 45
Sesno, Frank, 8
Shalala, Donna, 14
Shales, Tom, 8
Shaw, Bernard, 8
Shriver, Eunice/Sargeant, 46
Shriver, Mark K., **27,** 46
Simon, Paul, 28, *ill. 28*
Simpson, Alan, 28
Simpson, Donnie, 38
Snowe, Olympia, 28
Stallone, Sylvester, 46
Stenholm, Charles, 28

Stephanopoulos, George, 14
Stevens, John Paul, 28
Stewart, Potter, 46
Strauss, Robert, **28,** 36
Sullivan, Brendan V. Jr., 28
Tagliabue, Paul, 38
Talbott, Strobe, 14
Tauber, Laszlo, 38
Taylor, Elizabeth, 46, *ill.* 46
Thomas, Clarence, 46, 57
Thomas, Helen, 8, 60
Thompson, Fred, 28
Thompson, John R., 38
Thompson, Lee, 8
Torricelli, Bob, 18, **28**
Totenberg, Nina, 9, *ill.* 9
Tracht, Doug "Greaseman", 46
Trachtenberg, Steve, 29
Tyson, Mike, 38
Valenti, Jack, 9
Vance, Jim, 9
Wallop, Malcolm, 29
Walsh, Elsa *see* Woodward, Bob
Warner, John, 29: *see also* Taylor, Elizabeth
Waxman, Henry, 29
Webster, William, 47
Weinberger, Caspar, 29
Wertheimer, Fred/Linda, 9
White, Byron R., 47
Will, George, 9
Wolf, Warner, 47
Wolfensohn, James, 29
Woodward, Bob, **9,** 40, 41, 42, **47**
Woolsey, James, 47
Wouk, Herman, 9
Young, Don, 29

NEIGHBORHOOD INDEX

WASHINGTON, DC

ADAMS-MORGAN
CELEBRITIES
Bernstein, Carl, 40
Cooke, Janet, 42
Hitchens, Christopher, 4
Mankiewicz, Frank, 6
Woodward, Bob, 47
RESTAURANTS
Andalusian Dog, 55
Cafe Atlantico, 55
Cafe Lautrec, 56
Herb's Restaurant, 58
Millie & Al's, 59
Veneziano, 62

AMERICAN UNIVERSITY PARK
CELEBRITIES
Lake, Anthony, 13

BARNABY WOODS
CELEBRITIES
Brown, Ron, 12

BRIGHTWOOD
CELEBRITIES
Hughes, Cathy, 4

CARDOZA
RESTAURANTS
Florida Avenue Grill, 57

CAPITOL HILL
CELEBRITIES
Breaux, John, 16
Campbell, Ben Nighthorse, 17
Domenici, Pete, 19
Gingrich, Newt, 20
Gonzalez, Henry, 20
Gore, Al Sr., 20
Gorton, Slade, 21

(CAPITOL HILL CELEBRITIES *cont.*)
Hart, Gary, 43
Haskell, Floyd: *see* Totenberg, Nina
Heflin, Howell, 21
Jeffords, James, 22
Kamber, Vic, 22
Levin, Carl, 24
Lott, Trent, 24
Michel, Robert H., 25
Norton, Eleanor Holmes, 25
Pressler, Larry, 26
Snowe, Olympia, 28
Totenberg, Nina, 9
RESTAURANTS
Bullfeathers of Capitol Hill, 55
Hawk & Dove Restaurant, 58
La Brasserie, 59
La Colline, 59
Monocle On Capitol Hill, 59
Red River Grill, 61

CHEVY CHASE
CELEBRITIES
Cisneros, Henry, 12
Dellums, Ronald, 18
Matthews, Chris/Kathleen, 6
Sasser, James, 27

CLEVELAND PARK
CELEBRITIES
Albright, Madeline, 11
Bradley, Bill, 16
Buckley, Chris, 2
Edelman, Marian Wright, 19
Graham, Donald, 3
Hersh, Seymour, 3
Hollings, Ernest, 21
Lehrer, Jim, 5
Orth, Maureen, 6
Riley, Richard, 13
Russell, Mark, 38
Russert, Tim: *see* Orth, Maureen
Schorr, Daniel, 8
Wertheimer, Fred/Linda, 9

COLONIAL VILLAGE
CELEBRITIES
Jarvis, Charlene Drew, 22
Kelly, Sharon Pratt, 22

CONGRESS HEIGHTS
CELEBRITIES
Barry, Marion, 15

CRESTWOOD
CELEBRITIES
Rangel, Charles, 26
Rockefeller, John D./Sharon P., 27
Thompson, John R., 38

DOWNTOWN
CELEBRITIES
Alexander, Jane, 11
Aristide, Jean-Bertrand, 15
Baker, Howard, 15
Coverdell, Paul, 18
Friedan, Betty, 3
Kennedy, Joseph P. Jr., 23
Langhart, Janet, 35
Moynihan, Patrick, 25
Reno, Janet, 13
Rubin, Bob, 14
Thompson, Fred, 28
Torricelli, Bob, 28
RESTAURANTS
Bombay Club Restaurant, 55
Capital Bar at the Capital Hotel, 56
The Capital Grille, 56
Coco Loco, 57
Galileo Restaurant, 57
Georgia Brown's, 58
The Improv, 58
Jaleo, 58
Kinkead's Restaurant, 59
Mr. K's Restaurant, 60
My Brother's Place, 60
Old Ebbitt Grill, 60

DUPONT CIRCLE
CELEBRITIES
Pryor, David, 26
Stephanopoulos, George, 14
RESTAURANTS
City Lights of China, 56
Nora Restaurant, 60
Palm Restaurant, 61
Pizzeria Paradiso, 61
Sesto Senso, 61

FOGGY BOTTOM
CELEBRITIES
Davis, Evelyn Y., 33
Dole, Elizabeth/Robert, 18
Edwards, Don, 19
Foley, Mark, 19
Ginsburg, Ruth Bader, 20
Greenspan, Alan, 21
Kristol, Irving, 5
Lusk, Rufus, 35
Mars, Jackie, 36
Merrill, Philip, 6
Strauss, Robert, 28
Warner, John, 29
Weinberger, Caspar, 29

FOREST HILLS
CELEBRITIES
Brimmer, Andrew F., 17
Downie, Leonard, 3
Hoover, J. Edgar, 43
Johnson, Robert L., 34
McGovern, George, 44
Rivlin, Alice, 13
Rowan, Carl, 7

FOXHALL
CELEBRITIES
Baker, James, 40
Metzenbaum, Howard, 24
Murrow, Edward R., 45
Valenti, Jack, 9

FOXHALL VILLAGE
CELEBRITIES
Jordan, Vernon E. Jr., 22

GEORGETOWN

CELEBRITIES
Apple, A.W. "Johnny", 1
Aspin, Les, 39
Bingham, Joan, 31
Blatty, William Peter, 40
Bono, Sonny, 16
Bradlee, Ben, 1
Brock, David, 2
Brown, J. Carter, 31
Bruce, Evangeline, 31
Cafritz, Calvin, 32
Colby, William, 42
Cutler, Lloyd, 18
Evans, Rowland, 3
Graham, Katharine, 3
Harriman, Pamela, 12
Houghton, Amory Jr., 21
Hume, Brit, 4
Kelley, Kitty, 4
Kennedy, Jack/Jackie, 43
Kraft, Polly: see Cutler, Lloyd
Mellon, Paul, 36
Pell, Claiborne, 26
Percy, Charles, 26
Phillips, Laughlin, 37
Quinn, Sally: see Bradlee, Ben
Salinger, Pierre, 8
Shalala, Donna, 14
Taylor, Elizabeth, 46
Walsh, Elsa: see Woodward, Bob
Woodward, Bob, 9
Wouk, Herman, 9

RESTAURANTS
Blues Alley, 55
Cafe Milano, 56
Clyde's of Georgetown, 57
Fetoosh Restaurant, 57
Germaine's Asian Cuisine, 58
Morton's of Chicago-The Steakhouse, 60
Saigon Inn, 61
Sequoia Restaurant, 61

KALORAMA HEIGHTS
CELEBRITIES
Baldrige, Letitia, 1
Bentsen, Lloyd, 16
Boggs, Lindy, 16
Coyne, Marshall, 33
De Borchgrave, Arnaud, 2
Feinstein, Dianne, 19
Foley, Tom, 19
Haft, Herbert, 34
Haft, Robert, 34
Haft, Ronald, 34
Horne, Lena, 34
Kassebaum, Nancy, 22
Leach, Jim, 24
McNamara, Robert, 44
Raskin, Barbara, 7
Regardie, Bill, 7
Schieffer, Bob, 8
Trachtenberg, Steve, 29
Wolfensohn, James, 29
RESTAURANTS
Jockey Club Restaurant, 59

LAMOND RIGGS
CELEBRITIES
Ray, John, 26

LEDROIT PARK
CELEBRITIES
Jackson, Jesse, 22

MASSACHUSETTS HEIGHTS
CELEBRITIES
Cooke, Jack Kent, 32
Frist, Bill, 19
Kogod, Robert, 35
Lehrman, Samuel M., 35
Ourisman, Mandell, 37

NAVY YARD
RESTAURANTS
Tracks DC, 62

PALISADES
CELEBRITIES
Babbitt, Bruce, 11
Bork, Robert, 40
Cafritz, Conrad/Peggy, 32
Duffey, Joseph, 12
Hechinger, John W., 34
Kantor, Mickey, 12
Mitchell, Andrea, 6
Stewart, Potter, 46

SPRING VALLEY
CELEBRITIES
Berezden, Richard, 40
Bingaman, Jeff, 16
Bond, Christopher (Kit), 16
Carr, Robert O., 32
Danforth, John, 18
Johnson, Lyndon/Lady Bird, 43
Nixon, Pat/Richard, 45
Sullivan, Brendan V., 28
Vance, Jim, 9
Wallop, Malcolm, 29
RESTAURANTS
Wagshal's Delicatessen, 62

TENLEY
CELEBRITIES
Casey, William, 41
Gramm, Phil/Wendy, 21
RESTAURANTS
Austin Grill, 55

WATERFRONT
CELEBRITIES
Powell, Lewis F. Jr., 45
Simon, Paul, 28

WESLEY HEIGHTS
CELEBRITIES
Allbritton, Joseph, 31
Buchwald, Art, 2
Cafritz, Carter, 32
Glickman, Dan, 12
Helms, Richard, 43
Huffington, Arianna/Michael, 4
Marriott, Alice, 35
Nixon, Pat/Richard, 45
Packwood, Bob, 45
Povich, Shirley, 7

WOODLEY PARK
CELEBRITIES
Agnew, Spiro, 39
McClendon, Sarah, 6
O'Rourke, P.J., 6
Talbott, Strobe, 14
Thomas, Helen, 8

MARYLAND

BETHESDA
CELEBRITIES
Blitzer, Wolf, 1
Bumpers, Dale, 17
Carr, Oliver T., 32
Clifford, Clark, 17
Exon, J. James, 19
Ford, Wendell, 19
Haft, Gloria, 33
Haft, Linda, 33
Inouye, Daniel, 22
Kemp, Jack, 23
Kendall, David, 12
Koop, C. Everett, 44
Limpert, Jack, 6
Morella, Connie/Tony, 25
Nunn, Sam, 25
Oberstar, James, 26
Perry, William J., 13
Pollin, Abe, 37
Roberts, Cokie/Steve, 17
Scowcroft, Brent, 45
Shriver, Mark K., 27
Tagliabue, Paul, 38
Tyson, Mike, 38
Waxman, Henry, 29
Webster, William, 47
RESTAURANTS
The Original Pancake House, 60

CHEVY CHASE
CELEBRITIES
Bainum, Stewart Jr., 31
Bennett, Bill, 15
Boggs, Thomas, 16
Brinkley, David, 2
Kinsley, Michael, 5
O'Leary, Hazel, 13
Peterson, Gordon, 7
Safire, William, 7

(CHEVY CHASE CELEBRITIES, *cont.*)
Saul, B. Francis II, 38
Will, George, 9
Woolsey, James, 47

CLINTON
CELEBRITIES
Merkerson, S. Epatha, 37

DISTRICT HEIGHTS
CELEBRITIES
Hoyer, Steny, 21

KENSINGTON
CELEBRITIES
Mundy, Ken, 45

POOLESVILLE
CELEBRITIES
Kiplinger, Austin, 5

POTOMAC
CELEBRITIES
Altman, Robert, 15
Anderson, Jack, 1
Carter, Linda: *see* Altman, Robert
Dell, Donald, 33
Dikembe, Mutombo, 33
Downey, Edward M., 3
Ewing, Patrick, 33
Feld, Kenneth, 33
Kessler, Ron/Pamela, 4
Koppel, Ted, 5
Leonard, Sugar Ray, 44
Lewis, Delano, 5
Marriott, Bill, 35-36
Marriott, Richard, 36
Mourning, Alonzo, 37
Shaw, Bernard, 8
Shriver, Eunice/Sargeant, 46
Simpson, Donnie, 38
Stallone, Sylvester, 46
Tauber, Laszlo, 38
Thompson, Lee, 8
Tracht, Doug "Greaseman", 46
Wolf, Warner, 47
RESTAURANTS
Chicken-Out Rotisserie, 56

NEIGHBORHOOD INDEX
VIRGINIA

ALEXANDRIA
CELEBRITIES
Akaka, Daniel, 15
Cacheris, Plato, 17
Clinger, William F. Jr., 18
Cochran, Thad, 18
Ford, Betty/Jerry, 42
McCain, John, 24
Pena, Federico, 13
Roberts, Pat, 27
Schroeder, Pat, 27
RESTAURANTS
Fleetwood's Restaurant and Blues Club, 57

ARLINGTON
CELEBRITIES
Ames, Aldrich, 39
Beatty, Warren, 40
Boren, David, 16
Brennan, William Joseph, 41
Broder, David, 2
Bullock, Sandra, 41
Burger, Warren, 41
Couric, Katie, 42
Gore, Al/Tipper, 42
Helms, Jesse, 21
King, Larry, 4
Lamb, Brian P., 24
MacLaine, Shirley: see Beatty, Warren
Mars, Forrest E. Jr., 36
Meyers, Jan, 24
Obey, David, 26
Ray, Elizabeth, 45
Rehnquist, William, 45
Stenholm, Charles, 28
Stevens, John Paul, 28

ASBURN
CELEBRITIES
Green, Darrell, 33

FAIRFAX
CELEBRITIES
McCarthy, Eugene, 44
Thomas, Clarence, 46

89

FALLS CHURCH
CELEBRITIES
Marshall, Thurgood, 44

GREAT FALLS
CELEBRITIES
Gephardt, Richard, 20
Young, Don, 29

LEESBURG
CELEBRITIES
Baker, Russell, 1

MANHASSAS
CELEBRITIES
Bobbitt, John/Lorena, 40

MCLEAN
CELEBRITIES
Bennett, Bob, 15
Billington, James, 11
Buchanan, Patrick, 2
Brzezinski, Zbigniew, 41
Carlucci, Frank, 17
Chafee, John, 17
Cheney, Lynne/Richard, 17
Cuomo, Andrew/Kerry Kennedy, 12
Deconcini, Dennis, 18
Donaldson, Sam, 2
Dorgan, Byron, 19
Gergen, David, 20
Grosvenor, Gilbert M., 3
Haig, Alexander, 43
Johnston, J. Bennett Jr., 22
Kennedy, Anthony, 23
Kennedy, Ethel, 43
Kennedy, Joseph P. Jr., 23
Kennedy, Ted, 23
Kristol, William, 23
Lugar, Richard, 24
Meese, Ed III, 44
Monk, Art, 37
Noto, Lou, 37
Powell, Colin, 26
Reid, Harry, 27
Robb, Chuck/Lynda, 27
Scalia, Antonin, 27
Shales, Tom, 8
Simpson, Alan, 28
White, Byron R., 47

MT. VERNON
CELEBRITIES
Jurgensen, Sonny, 34

RESTON
CELEBRITIES
Sesno, Frank, 8

STERLING
CELEBRITIES
Casserly, Charley, 32

VIENNA
CELEBRITIES
Hatch, Orrin, 21
LaPierre, Wayne R., 24
Nickles, Don, 25